Tackling Numeracy Issues
Book 6

Improving the plenary session Years 3 and 4

Caroline Clissold

A *Questions* book for teachers

Tackling Numeracy Issues
Book 6

Improving the plenary session
Years 3 and 4

Caroline Clissold

The *Questions* Publishing Company Limited
Birmingham
2002

The Questions Publishing Company Ltd
Leonard House, 321 Bradford Street, Digbeth, Birmingham B5 6ET

First published in 2002

ISBN: 1-84190-077-X

Design and incidental illustration by Ivan Morison
Cover by Martin Cater

Printed in the UK

Also available from the Questions Publishing Company Limited:

Book 1 *Fractions and Decimals, Key Stage 1*
ISBN: 1-84190-079-6

Book 2 *Fractions, Decimals and Percentages, Key Stage 2*
ISBN: 1-84190-047-8

Book 3 *Fractions, Decimals, Percentages, Ratio and Proportion, Key Stage 2, Years 5 and 6*
ISBN: 1-84190-048-6

Book 4 *Solving Maths Word Problems*
ISBN: 1-84190-052-4

Book 5 *Improving the Plenary Session, Key Stage 1, Years 1 and 2*
ISBN: 1-84190-053-2

Book 7 *Improving the Plenary Session, Key Stage 2, Years 5 and 6*
ISBN: 1-84190-078-8

Contents

Introduction

According to Ofsted's report *The National Numeracy Strategy: An Interim Evaluation by HMI*, the plenary is the 'least successful element of the daily Maths lesson'. HMI stated that a typical problem was 'poor time management in the other elements of the lesson which meant that the time originally allocated to the plenary was lost.' The report stressed that the best plenary sessions are used to 'draw together the key ideas of the lesson, reinforce teaching points made earlier, assess what has been understood and correct errors and misconceptions.'

The plenary is designed to round off the maths lesson, with the class coming together as a whole. It should take between 10 and 15 minutes. Initially, you may have to make a big effort to make adequate time for a plenary. However, it soon becomes second nature.

This book focuses on how to improve the plenary part of your numeracy lessons. It gives basic lesson ideas, based on objectives from the National Numeracy Strategy's Framework for Teaching Mathematics. These will need developing and differentiating to suit your particular class. Each lesson idea comes with detailed suggestions for a suitable plenary session.

There are many ways in which the plenary part of the maths lesson can be executed. Here are some suggestions, most of which will be expanded on in this book:

- ✪ Ask the children to present and explain their work.
- ✪ Celebrate success in the children's work.
- ✪ Discuss what was the easiest/hardest/most enjoyable part of the lesson.
- ✪ Make a note of any successes and/or misconceptions to be dealt with at the time or during the next lesson. If common misconceptions are discovered during the lesson, it might be helpful to shorten the lesson and increase the plenary time to deal with these.
- ✪ Mark a written exercise done individually during the lesson, so that you can question the children appropriately and assess their work.
- ✪ Discuss and compare the efficiency of children's methods of working out a calculation.
- ✪ Help the children to generalise a rule from examples generated by different groups.
- ✪ Draw together what has been learned; reflect on what was important in the lesson; summarise key facts, ideas and vocabulary and what needs to be remembered.
- ✪ Play a fun game relevant to the maths learnt during the lesson.
- ✪ At the end of a unit of work, draw together what has been learnt over a series of lessons.
- ✪ Link skills that have been learned to problem solving within a context relevant to the children.

✪ Discuss what pupils will do next as a progression from the present lesson.
✪ Consolidate and develop what has been learnt. For example, if the lesson was about numbers on a number square, review the objectives and develop them further, extending the activity with larger numbers.
✪ Make links to work in other maths topics or other subjects.
✪ Set homework or a challenge to be done out of class.

It must be stressed that each activity needs to be related to the objective of the lesson.

Variety is essential. The same type of plenary will soon become tedious for both yourself and the children. It is therefore important that different aspects are covered during each week. All sessions, of course, will involve assessment of varying degrees.

There are a few important things to remember:

✪ Have a clear plan in mind of what you want to achieve during the plenary.
✪ Make sure you leave enough time for it.
✪ Ensure that the children know if they are to present something during the plenary, so that they can prepare for it.
✪ At the end of the plenary make a general evaluation of the lesson's success and how the children have worked.
✪ Have a definite routine at the end of a lesson to mark its finish; this is particularly relevant for the younger children.

Topics and objectives

Chapter 1 Presentation and explanation of the children's work
Ideas for plenary sessions that give selected groups of children opportunities for showing and explaining their work to the rest of the class, based on lesson ideas which have the following objectives:

Year 3 objectives
Describe and extend number sequences.
Understand and use the vocabulary of estimation; give sensible estimates
Recognise and find simple fractions and equivalencies.
Develop paper and pencil methods for additions that cannot be done mentally.
Solve word problems involving numbers in real life using one or more steps.
Suggest and use simple measuring equipment, reading and interpreting number scales with some accuracy.
Know and use units of time and the relationship between them; read the time from clocks.
Know what a right angle is.

Year 4 objectives:
Recognise and order negative numbers.
Recognise multiples and know some test of divisibility.
Use fraction notation and recognise the equivalence between fractions.
Use a variety of mental calculation strategies to solve calculations and decide which is the most efficient.
Use all four operations to solve 3D shapes; classify them according to their properties.
Recognise translations in patterns.
Make and measure clockwise and anti-clockwise turns.

Chapter 2 Progression — where are we going next?
Ideas for plenary session which will highlight where the work the children have been doing will lead for the next lesson, based on lesson ideas which have the following objectives:

Years 3 objectives:
Use and apply knowledge of adding and subtracting 1 or 10 in a variety of ways.
Understand that addition can be done in any order.
Understand the principle that subtraction reverses addition.
Use knowledge of doubles and halves to multiple or divide.
Solve simple one-step word problems set in real-life contexts and explain how the problem was solved.
Suggest suitable units to estimate or measure capacity.
Make shapes and patterns with increasing accuracy, and describe their features.
Describe and find the position of a square on a grid.

Year 4 objectives:
Read and write whole numbers; know what each digit in a number represents.
Multiple and divide whole numbers by 10.
Use decimal notation; know what each digit in a decimal fraction represents.
Use doubling and halving to multiply and divide by 4.
Give a remainder as a whole number.
Estimate and measure lengths with increasing accuracy to the nearest centimetre.
Measure and calculate the perimeter of simple shapes.
Recognise positions and directions, and use co-ordinates.

Chapter 3 Links to other maths topics and curriculum areas

Numeracy and literacy:	Year 3
	Year 4
Numeracy and science:	Teeth and eating
	Growth of plants
	Moving and growing
	Habitats
Numeracy and history:	A Roman case study
	An Anglo-Saxon case study
Numeracy and geography:	Investigating the local area
	The school environment
Numeracy and art:	Investigating pattern
Numeracy and PE:	Directions
Other areas of maths	

Chapter 4 Problem solving and games

Visualising
Acting out problems
Making up problems
Games

Chapter 5 Other ideas for an effective plenary

Analysing the lesson
Identifying misconceptions
Generalising rules
Reflection, summarising and consolidation
Celebrating success

Chapter 1
Presentation and explanation of the children's work

When the National Numeracy Strategy was first put into place in primary schools, many teachers felt that this aspect of the lesson was not really important. In a lot of cases there was no time left for it at the end of the lesson, or if there was, the plenary consisted of a quick 'let's see what this group have done today' or the show and tell approach.

In my observations of lessons I still meet with teachers who say such things as:
"I don't want to stop the children when they are working so hard."
"Oh dear, I ran out of time."
"I'm not very good at plenaries, so I tend not to do them."
Happily, I meet far more teachers these days who are increasingly seeing the importance and value of the plenary part of the lesson, and use it confidently with a valid purpose.

At the beginning of the plenary it is always important to refer to the objectives of the lesson. If you are using the explaining and presenting approach, the selected group of children/pairs/individuals will need to be able to tell the other children in the class what they have been doing, how it has helped them understand or has reinforced the objectives from the main teaching activity and whether they feel they have been successful.

It can be counter productive to ask the children to explain what they have been doing and how they got on during the plenary without prior warning. Doing so can cause embarrassment and anxiety in some children. It can also lack focus and quite frankly be a waste of ten minutes. The children need to be told in advance that they will be asked to talk about their work and how it has helped them achieve the lesson objectives, so that they can be prepared.

If you have a teaching assistant, it might be worth considering asking them to help the group they are working with to plan their plenary activity The teaching assistant does not necessarily need to work with the less able group always. Remember that it is the teacher's responsibility to teach that group at least once or twice a week. On these occasions you might ask your assistant to work with other children to help them with their presentation skills. Some children will welcome this help, as presenting and explaining work without a real focus can be very daunting to some, even the most able.

It is helpful to have a selection of appropriate questions that you might ask the children during the plenary, for example:

✪ What activity have you been doing during this session?
✪ Can you explain why you have been doing this?
✪ Has it helped you achieve the objectives?
✪ What do you know now that you didn't before?

Year 3

1. Counting in steps

> **Objective:** Describe and extend number sequences: count on or back in steps of any size
> **Strand:** Numbers and the number system
> **Topic:** Counting, properties of numbers and number sequences

Paired activity
Looking at patterns when counting on in different steps from different numbers on a number square.

Begin by counting on and back in twos, threes and fours from given numbers. Show the children a hundred square (see photocopiable sheet 1) and ask them what pattern they think they will get if they colour all the even numbers; start on 1 and colour in steps of two; start on 3 and colour in steps of three, etc.
Give each pair four 5 by 5 grids and instruction cards. See photocopiable sheet 2.

Make available some 6 x 6 number grids for the same instruction cards. What do they notice? Can the children think of an explanation as to why this happens?

Plenary
Refer to the objectives! Choose four pairs to come to the front of the class to demonstrate and explain to the rest of the children what they noticed about the patterns from the four question cards. Ask them to tell everyone why they think the patterns are as they are. Choose another pair to demonstrate the 6 x 6 grid patterns. Use a 6 x 6 acetate, counters and an OHP for this because it will be clearer for those who did not manage the task in the lesson.

2. Estimating and rounding

> **Objective:** Understand and use the vocabulary of estimation; give sensible estimates
> **Strand:** Numbers and the number system
> **Topic:** Estimating and rounding

Group activity
Estimating the position of a point on a number line.

Begin by drawing some number lines on the board from 0 to 10, 10 to 20, 30 to 40, etc. and ask the children to come to the front and mark on where certain numbers should go.

Example

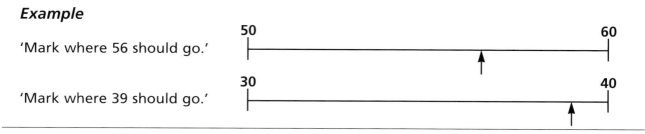

'Mark where 56 should go.'

'Mark where 39 should go.'

Give the groups some number lines with marks already on them. The children need to estimate what the numbers are.

Example

0   100

Plenary
Refer to the objectives! The selected group should come to the front and explain how they worked out what each of their numbers were. They need to have access to a number line, maybe drawn by you on the board, so that they can demonstrate effectively. Ask the rest of the class to make comments. Do they agree with the group? What other number could they have estimated and why?

3. Fractions

> **Objective:** Recognise and find simple fractions and equivalences between them
> **Strand:** Numbers and the number system
> **Topic:** Fractions

Group activity
Recognising halves, quarters, fifths and tenths and their equivalences.

Use an OHP for an initial demonstration. Prepare a blank rectangle that can house halves, quarters, fifths and tenths and smaller pieces to represent those fractions.
Fit the sections into the rectangle to show that 2 halves = the whole, 4 quarters = the whole, 5 fifths = the whole and 10 tenths = the whole.
Then demonstrate, using individual pieces, that $\frac{1}{2} = \frac{2}{4}$, $\frac{1}{2} = \frac{5}{10}$ and $\frac{2}{10} = \frac{1}{5}$.

Give the groups some paper; ask them to cut out pieces as you have (they may need templates for the whole and tenths for accuracy). Then ask them to order them from smallest to largest and record. Ask other questions such as: What two fractions are equivalent to $\frac{3}{4}$? How many tenths are the same as $\frac{4}{5}$?

Plenary
Refer to the objectives! Invite some groups to demonstrate what they have been doing. The first group could show the ordering, explaining how they knew where to put the pieces. Another two or three could explain how they worked out the answers to the equivalences.

4. Pencil and paper calculations

> **Objective:** Develop pencil and paper methods for additions that cannot, at this stage, be done mentally
> **Strand:** Calculations
> **Topic:** Pencil and paper procedures (addition)

Paired activity

Addition using a number line, counting on in multiples of 100, 10 or 1.

Demonstrate this pencil and paper method first:

37 + 25

$$
\frac{\qquad \overset{+\,20}{} \qquad \overset{+\,3}{} \qquad \overset{+\,2}{} \qquad}{37 \qquad\qquad 57 \qquad\qquad 60 \qquad\qquad 62}
$$

Then demonstrate how this can be written without the line: 37 + 20 + 3 + 2 = 62.
Give the pairs of children some calculations (differentiated of course) to work on.

Plenary

Refer to the objectives! Ask some of the pairs of children to come to the board and demonstrate what they have been doing, explaining each step carefully and clearly.

5. Two-step problems

> **Objective:** Solve word problems involving numbers in 'real life' using one or more steps. Explain how the problem was solved
> **Strand:** Solving problems
> **Topic:** 'Real-life' problems

Group activity

Solving simple two-step problems set in 'real-life' contexts and explaining how the problem was solved.

Remind the children that there are four basic steps to problem solving:

1. Understand the problem (find and identify the key pieces of information that you need to put together to get the answer).
2. Explore the problem (choose the necessary operation or operations to use to solve it).
3. Solve the problem (solve the problem and get an answer).
4. Check the solution (check the children's work for possible errors and ensure that they have actually answered the question).

Examples

Work through some two-step problems, similar to the ideas below, with the children.

1. Mick bought eight packs of football cards. In each pack there were ten cards. He gave 35 stickers to his best friend.
   How many cards did he have left?

2. There were 100 pears on the pear tree. My friend picked 29 and I picked 37.
   How many were left on the tree?

Give each group a selection of problems to work through and ask them to make up some of their own, which they can have a go at acting out. Tell one group that they will be acting out their problem for the others in the plenary.

Plenary

Refer to the objectives! The 'selected group' act out the scenario of the problem they make up or one you give to them, and ask the rest of the class to solve it.

Example

Three children go into a shop; they each buy a book costing £2.50. One of the children pays for them all, with a £10 note, and is given change.
Four children act this out; another one explains their actions. The rest of the class need to work out how much change is given and explain ways in which the problem can be solved.

6. Measuring

> **Objective:** Suggest and use simple measuring equipment, reading and interpreting number scales with some accuracy
> **Strand:** Measures
> **Topic:** Length, mass and capacity

Group activity

Using calibrated scales to measure different items, estimating first.

Demonstrate the group activity by modelling what you expect the children to do. Ask some volunteers to help you. Estimate the weights of the items against 1kg, 500g and 100g weights. Weigh them and see how close your estimate was.
Give each group a table, similar to the one below, to complete:

Object	Estimated weight	Actual weight	Difference

> **Now order your objects from lightest to heaviest along this number line:**
> _____

Plenary

Refer to the objectives! Choose one of the groups to demonstrate exactly what they did during their 'working independently' session. Ask them to explain clearly such things as how they made their estimates, whether their estimates got more accurate the more attempts they made and how they read the scales accurately.

7. Time

Objective: Know and use units of time and the relationships between them; read the time from clocks
Strand: Measures
Topic: Time

Group activity
Matching digital and analogue clock times.

Begin with a whole-class introduction, the children using their own individual clocks. Call out clock times for them to make, ensuring that the hour hand is in the correct place. Make some of the times you call out analogue and others digital so that they have to convert from one to the other.
Ask them to show you the answers to simple problems, for example: "My clock shows 3:00. It is 15 minutes slow. What is the real time?"
Give small groups of children some time 'snap' cards, to use in a game. Tell them that before they can complete their 'snap' they must also find the time on the clock.

Example

12:30	Half past 12
7:35	25 minutes to 8
2:10	10 minutes past 2

Plenary
Refer to the objectives! Ask some of the pairs of children to show their 'snaps'. They need to tell everyone what each time actually means, e.g. 2:10 is 10 minutes past 2; 3:45 is 45 minutes past 3 or 15 minutes to 4. They should also show the clock times on their clock faces.

8. Right angles

Objective: Know what a right angle is
Strand: Shape and space
Topic: Movement and angle

Group activity
Sorting 2-D shapes according to whether they have all, some or no right angles.

Remind the children what a right angle is. Ask them to tell you some objects in the classroom that have them. Give them a piece of paper and ask them to fold it into an irregular shape. Has it any right angles? How many? Repeat this two or three times.
Give each group a selection of 2-D shapes to sort into a table similar to the one below:

All right angles	Some right angles	No right angles

Plenary

Refer to the objectives! Ask one of the groups to show their shapes, name them and tell the others how many right angles they have. If they can use an OHP, this will make their demonstration more effective.

Year 4

9. Negative numbers

Objective: Recognise and order negative numbers
Strand: Numbers and the number system
Topic: Negative numbers

Paired activity

Using negative numbers in the context of temperature.

Begin by finding out what the children know about negative numbers, i.e. what they are, when they would see them. Give each child a number line from –15 to 15.
See photocopiable sheet 3.

Ask the children to use their number lines to follow your instructions, e.g. "Begin on 0, move up 5, down 6, up 12, down 10. What number are you on?" "Begin on 7, move down 3, down 8, up 15, up 3, down 16. What number are you on?"
Put some numbers on the board. Ask the children to draw their own number lines and order the numbers from lowest to highest.

Demonstrate the use of a thermometer.
In their pairs, give the children the pictures of thermometers on photocopiable sheet 4 and ask them to read the temperatures.
If the temperature rises by two degrees, what will the temperatures show on each thermometer?
If the temperature drops by two degrees, what will the temperature show on each thermometer?

Plenary

Refer to the objectives! Ask pairs of children to talk about their work, possibly demonstrating by drawing (or asking you to draw) thermometers on the board.
They need to explain how they worked out those temperatures that did not come against a mark. Ask them to show how they calculated the answers to the two questions.

10. Multiples and divisibility

Objective: Recognise multiples and know some tests of divisibility
Strand: Numbers and the number system
Topic: Properties of numbers

Group activity

Investigating tests of divisibility for the 2, 3, 4, 5 and 10 times tables.

Write up the answers to times-tables facts from 1 x to 10 x. Ask the children what they notice about these numbers:

2 4 6 8 10 12 14 16 18 20 (all even, every other number in the number system)

3 6 9 12 15 18 21 24 27 30 (odd, even, odd, even pattern, digits add to 3, 6, or 9)

4 8 12 16 20 24 28 32 36 40 (all even, can be divided by 2 twice)

5 10 15 20 25 30 35 40 45 50 (all end in 5 or 0)

10 20 30 40 50 60 70 80 90 100 (all end in 0)

Put some numbers on the board. Can the children use these rules to work out if certain numbers can be divided by 2, 3, 4, 5 or 10 and are therefore multiples of those numbers? Give the groups some random numbers and ask them to sort them and describe how they did it.

Example

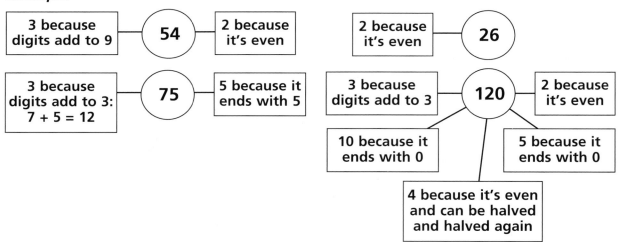

Ask the groups to find as many numbers as they can which can be divided by all five numbers.

Plenary

Refer to the objectives! Ask 'selected' groups to explain to the rest of the class how they worked out whether the numbers were multiples of 2, 3, 4, 5 or 10. Ask them to tell the others some of the numbers they made up themselves which can be divided by all the numbers and explain how they worked this out.

11. Fractions and equivalence

Objective: Use fraction notation and recognise the equivalence between fractions
Strand: Numbers and the number system
Topic: Fractions

Group activity

Finding the equivalences between halves, quarters and eighths and ordering them on a number line.

Example

One whole							
$\frac{1}{2}$							
$\frac{1}{4}$							
$\frac{1}{8}$							

Demonstrate by using strips like those above or something similar. They need to be prepared by you beforehand. The 'whole' strip should be made from card and the fraction parts coloured on acetate and cut up into their sections. You will need an OHP to make it effective. If you do not have access to an OHP you could adapt the idea using large pieces of paper.

Use the pieces of acetate to show how many halves, quarters and eighths make a whole, how many quarters and eighths make a half and how many eighths make a quarter.

Give each group some card and ask them to make their own strips and pieces like yours and investigate as many equivalences as they can.

Example

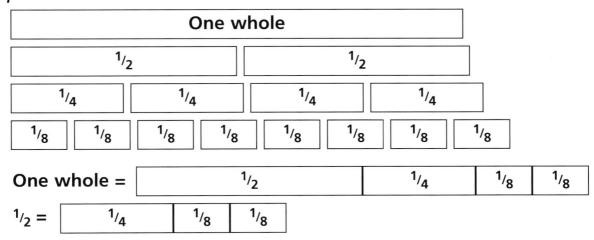

Plenary

Refer to the objectives! Invite one of the groups to demonstrate all the equivalences that they found. It would be a good idea to let them use the OHP and your acetate pieces for their demonstration.

---

12. Mental addition and subtraction

Objective: Use a variety of mental calculation strategies to solve calculations and decide which is the most efficient
Strand: Calculations
Topic: Mental calculation strategies (+ and -)

Group activity

Answering calculations in as many ways as possible and deciding which method is the best.

Begin by reminding the children of the strategies that they have learnt, i.e. partitioning into hundreds, tens and ones, identifying near doubles and adding/subtracting the nearest multiple and adjusting.
Demonstrate the group activity by writing a calculation on the board and asking the children to brainstorm their ideas for solving it:

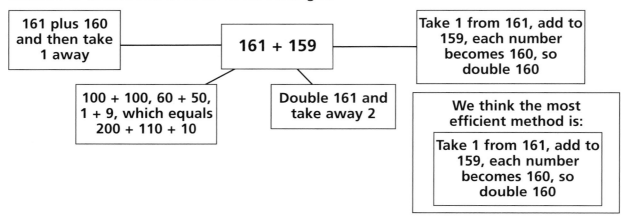

Give each group a variety of calculations to brainstorm in the same way.

Plenary

Refer to the objectives! Ask 'selected' groups to explain the strategies they used to answer the calculations that you gave them. Invite the rest of the class to give their opinions on the efficiency of each one and come to a class decision on which is the best to use.

13. Time problems

Objective: Use all four operations to solve word problems involving time
Strand: Solving problems
Topic: Problems involving time

Group activity

Solving 'story' problems involving units of time and explaining and recording how the problem was solved.

Demonstrate the group activity using acetates and an OHP. Put up a timetable similar to the following:

Bus stop	Bus 57	Bus 64	Bus 25
High Street	11:05		1:45
Church			
Post Office		1:05	
Sports Centre			

A bus takes 20 minutes between stops. Fill in the timetable.
Ask such questions as:
If the bus leaves the High Street at 11:15, what time should it arrive at the Sports Centre?
If the last bus gets to the Post Office four minutes early, what time does it arrive?
If Sue wants to play squash at 2:00, which bus must she catch?

Give each group a similar table to fill in and ask them to make up some questions to answer from it.

Plenary
Refer to the objectives! Ask the 'selected' group to show their completed timetable to the rest of the class and ask the other children the questions that they made up.

14. 2-D and 3-D shapes

> **Objective:** Describe and visualise 3-D shapes; classify them according to their properties
> **Strand:** Shape and space
> **Topic:** Properties of 3-D and 2-D shapes

Group activity
Describing 3-D shapes according to their properties using the correct vocabulary.

Show a selection of polyhedrons and ask the children to describe them using their knowledge that:

- ✪ Each face is a flat surface and is a polygon.
- ✪ An edge is the straight line where two faces meet.
- ✪ A vertex is the point where three or more edges meet.
- ✪ A prism has two identical end faces and the same cross-section throughout its length.

Give each group between eight and ten different shapes. Ask them to take it in turns to describe a shape to the others, then group them in sets according to criteria they choose themselves, e.g. no triangular faces/at least one triangular face.

Plenary
Refer to the objectives! Invite one of the groups to explain their work to the others and then to describe some of their shapes for the class to visualise and then name.

15. Reflective symmetry

> **Objective:** Recognise translations in patterns
> **Strand:** Shape and space
> **Topic:** Reflective symmetry, reflection and translation

Group activity
Making patterns by repeatedly translating a shape.

Demonstrate using shapes and an OHP, as shown below.

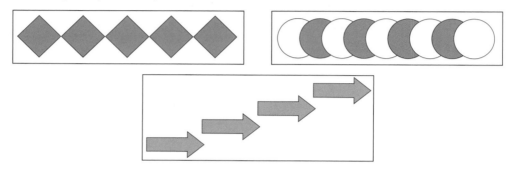

Give the children some card and a large piece of paper each. Ask them to make a simple shape each and then make a translation poster by drawing around it, moving it and drawing round it again and again.

Plenary
Refer to the objectives! Invite some children to demonstrate a translation by showing their posters and showing what they did by using the OHP and their original shape.

16. Angle and rotation

> **Objective:** Make and measure clockwise and anti-clockwise turns
> **Strand:** Shape and space
> **Topic:** Angle and rotation

Paired activity
Using clocks to make and measure (in degrees) clockwise and anticlockwise turns.

Each child will need a small cardboard/plastic clock. Photocopiable sheet 5 can be used and pasted onto card. Ask the children to put the hands on 12, and then move one hand to the 3. What kind of angle have they made? What is its size in degrees? Put both hands back on 12. Can they work out how many degrees it will be if they move one hand to 1 and then 2? How many degree turns are there between each of the numbers on the clock? For their paired activity, give the children a selection of cards with degrees written on and a number. Ask them to use their clocks, put the hands on the number shown and make the degree of turn stated with one hand, say the time the clock now shows and record their work.

Plenary

Refer to the objectives! Invite several of the pairs of children to demonstrate what they have been doing, involve the rest of the class, by choosing a card, asking the class to put the hands on the shown number and count round the correct number of degrees. Alter the hour hand so that it is in the correct position for the time and ask the class to show their clocks and tell the pair the time that they have.

Finish by asking the children to work out more complex turns, e.g. "Put both hands on the 12. What time would you get if you moved the hour hand round 270°?"

30^0	60^0	120^0	90^0
6	**7**	**2**	**10**

I put both hands on the 6 and move one round 30⁰. It landed on the 7. The time I made was half past 7.	I put both hands on the 7 and move one round 60⁰. It landed on the 9. The time I made was quarter to 7.	I put both hands on the 2 and move one round 120⁰. It landed on the 6. The time I made was half past 2.	I put both hands on the 10 and move one round 90⁰. It landed on the 1. The time I made was 10 minutes to 1.

Photocopiable Sheet 1
Hundred square

1	2	3	4	5	6	7	8	9	10
11	12	13	14	15	16	17	18	19	20
21	22	23	24	25	26	27	28	29	30
31	32	33	34	35	36	37	38	39	40
41	42	43	44	45	46	47	48	49	50
51	52	53	54	55	56	57	58	59	60
61	62	63	64	65	66	67	68	69	70
71	72	73	74	75	76	77	78	79	80
81	82	83	84	85	86	87	88	89	90
91	92	93	94	95	96	97	98	99	100

Photocopiable Sheet 2
Grid and instruction cards

1	2	3	4	5
6	7	8	9	10
11	12	13	14	15
16	17	18	19	20
21	22	23	24	25

1	2	3	4	5	6
7	8	9	10	11	12
13	14	15	16	17	18
19	20	21	22	23	24
25	26	27	28	29	30
31	32	33	34	35	36

1

Colour in the number 1.

Count on in threes and colour the numbers you land on.

What do you notice?

2

Colour in the number 2.

Count on in threes and colour the numbers you land on.

Do you get the same pattern?

What do you notice?

3

Colour in the number 25.

Count back in threes and colour the numbers you land on.

What do you notice?

4

Colour in the number 24.

Count back in threes and colour the numbers you land on.

How does this compare to the last card?

Photocopiable Sheet 3
Number line

Photocopiable Sheet 4
Temperatures

Photocopiable Sheet 5
Clock

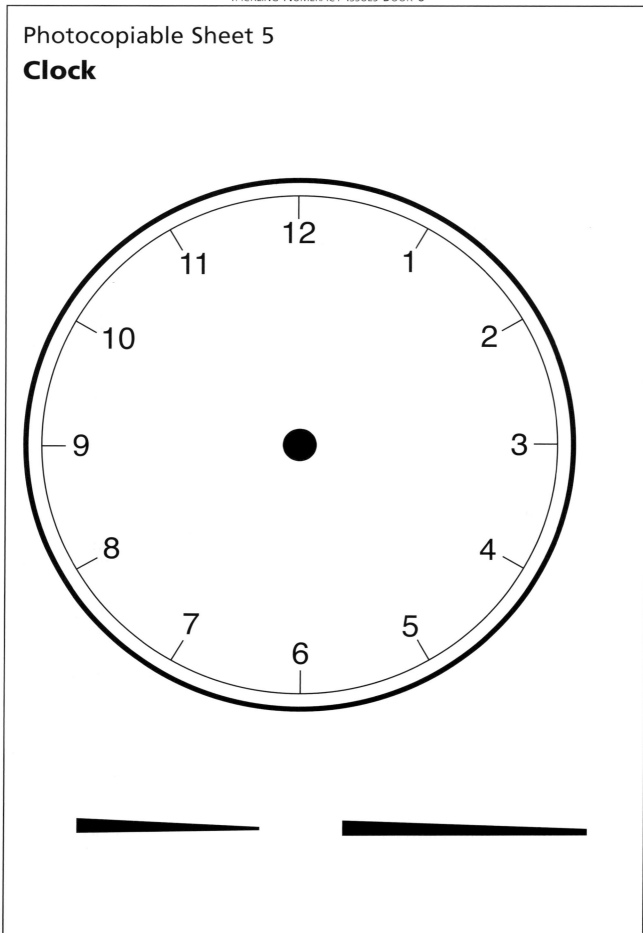

© The Questions Publishing Company Ltd

Chapter 2
Progression – where are we going next?

Put yourself inside the mind of a young child who has been asked to estimate a number of items. Their immediate reaction will probably be to think:

- ✪ I want to count them to find out exactly how many there are.
- ✪ I can count: why should I guess and maybe get it wrong?
- ✪ What is the point of estimating?
- ✪ I think I'll count and hope the teacher doesn't see me!

Does this sound familiar?

Estimating is a very good example of why it is important that the children know the purpose of what they are doing and where it will lead in the future. Estimating is a useful skill if the children need to know numbers and measurements in a practical context, for example:

- ✪ Will there be enough potatoes in this bag for our family to eat this Sunday?
- ✪ Will I have enough pennies to go to the shop to buy some sweets?

Estimating the answer first, answering and comparing the answer to the estimate is also important for calculation work. If they are close, the answer is likely to be correct and it will be worth a proper check.

This is the same in all areas of maths. It is important that the children know the 'whole picture' of what they are learning and why, so that they can see that it is relevant to them. Children always learn best if they can see why they are doing something. On occasions, during your plenary, tell the children how what they have learnt will help them during the next lesson.

This chapter aims to give lesson objectives from the NNS Framework for Teaching Mathematics, lesson ideas and a plenary outlining where the work the children have been doing will lead for the next lesson.

Remember to refer to the objective of the lesson taught initially and then inform the children of what they will be doing next time and why.

Year 3

1. Ordering numbers

Objective: Use and apply knowledge of adding and subtracting 1 or 10 in a variety of ways
Leading to: Using their knowledge to complete parts of a two-digit number square
Strand: Numbers and the number system
Topic: Place value and ordering

Paired activity

Responding to questions involving addition and subtraction of multiples of 10, and numbers ending with 9 and 11, more or less than given numbers.

Begin by showing the hundred square on photocopiable sheet 1, and asking the children questions such as: "What number is 10 more than 37?" , "30 less than 56?" , "19 more than 28?", "21 more than 16?" Ask the children how they worked the last two out, i.e. 20 more than 28 and then back 1; 20 more than 16 and one more on. Ask the children to imagine the square goes from 101 to 200. Ask such questions as: "What is 20 more than 134?", "40 less than 171?"

Give each pair of children two packs of cards, one with random two and three-digit numbers on and the second with instructions such as + 29, -11, +30. Ask them to turn one from each pack over, answer the calculation using an imaginary number square in their minds and record their method of working.

Example

23	+29

23 + 30 - 1 = 52

54	-30

54 - 30 = 24

87	-31

87 - 30 - 1 = 56

14	+79

14 + 80 - 1 = 93

66	+21

66 + 20 + 1 = 87

98	-39

98 - 40 + 1 = 59

Plenary

Discuss the strategies that the children used to work out the calculations they were given. Next, show a hundred square, as in photocopiable sheet 1, blank out some numbers and ask the children to tell you which they are and how they worked them out. Ask for as many possible ways as they can, e.g. A = 18, because it is one more than 17, one less than 19, 10 more than 8, 10 less than 28.

Tell the children that as they have done so well today, next time they will be looking at small parts of a number square and trying to work out which numbers are missing. Show them an example:

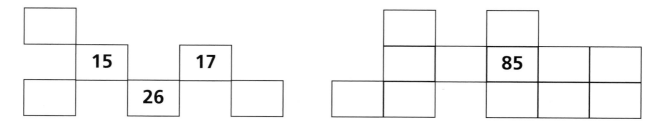

2. Addition

> **Objective:** Understand that addition can be done in any order
> **Leading to:** Checking answers by changing the order around
> **Strand:** Calculations
> **Topic:** Understanding addition

Paired activity

Looking at the best order to add a set of numbers.

Write some addition calculations on the board and brainstorm methods of answering.

Example

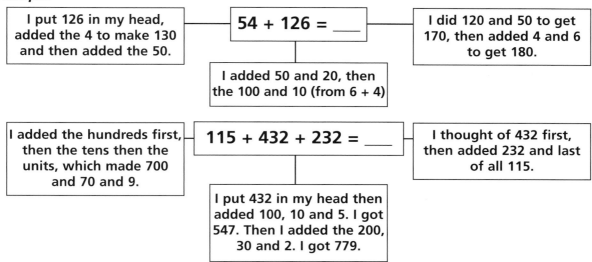

Ask the children how many of them worked with the highest number in their minds first. Ask them if it would make a difference if the numbers were added in a different order. Give the pairs of children calculations to answer, using whichever order they want. They need to record their work.

Plenary

Discuss the work the children have done. Ask them to show some of their methods, by writing what they did on the board.
Ask them if they can think of any reasons why it is useful to be able to add numbers in any order. Accept their replies. If not mentioned lead to the idea of being able to check answers. Write up an example.

Example

148 + 217 + 244 =
Ask someone to help you by adding as they would like to, e.g. 200 + 200 + 100 = 500, 40 + 10 + 40 = 90, 8 + 7 + 4 = 19, 500 + 90 + 19 = 609
Ask how they could check this answer. Hopefully, someone will suggest trying to add them in a different order, i.e. 244 + 217 + 148 or 217 + 148 + 244.

Tell the children that as they have been so successful today, they will be learning about estimating answers and checking next time.

3. Calculations

> **Objective:** Understand the principle that subtraction reverses addition
> **Leading to:** Use of inversions to help find missing numbers in calculations
> **Strand:** Calculations
> **Topic:** Understanding subtraction

Paired activity

Making up addition and subtraction number sentences.

Begin by writing three numbers on the board (they must be able to make an addition calculation)
e.g.   84   31 53
Ask the children to try to put these into number sentences using addition or subtraction:
31 + 53 = 84
53 + 31 = 83
84 – 31 = 53
84 – 53 = 31

Give the pairs of children cards with three numbers on, and ask them to make number sentences as you demonstrated.

Plenary

Ask some of the pairs to demonstrate their number sentences, explaining clearly what they are doing.
Tell the children that now they have grasped the concept of the same three numbers being put together in different ways to make four different calculations, they will be using this knowledge next time to help them work out missing number problems. Give an example:

34 + ☐ = 86

Ask how this can be solved and show the initial calculations you used during the demonstration as an aid. Write up the four number sentences that go with the above calculation, using a box for the missing number, and discuss how any might help solve the problem.

☐ + 34 = 86

34 + ☐ = 86

86 – 34 = ☐

86 – ☐ = 34

4. Mental calculations

> **Objective:** Use knowledge of doubles and halves to multiply or divide
> **Leading to:** Working out four times table facts by doubling the two timetable facts, and finding quarters by halving and halving again
> **Strand:** Calculations
> **Topic:** Mental calculation strategies (x and ÷)

Group activity

Linking doubling to the 2x table and halving to ÷ by 2, working out doubles and halves of numbers.

Introduce this by asking the children to use their digit cards to answer your questions. Ask such questions as "What is double 5?", "Double 16?", "Double 24?", "How did you work these out?", "What is half of 50?", "Half of 26?", "Half of 150?"
Ask the children to play a game such as the one below in groups of three or four.

The Halving Game
Help Martin down the ski slope
You need photocopiable sheet 7 for this game. Use digit cards to make up numbers. Digit cards are on photocopiable sheet 6. Each child chooses two cards and makes the highest number that they can. The idea of the game is to attempt to halve their number and keep it as a whole number. If they can, they move their counter along the game board one square; if they can't, the next player has their go. For example: Player 1 picks 4 and 3, so they must make 43 – they can't halve it and keep it as a whole number. Player 2 picks 7 and 4, so they must make 74 – they can halve it, so they move one place along the game board. The winner is the player who helps Martin down the ski slope!

Plenary
Discuss the game that the children have been playing. Did they find it easy to halve the numbers? What sort of strategies did they use? Did they enjoy playing it?' Who won?
Tell the children that next time they will be looking at multiplying by 4 by doubling and doubling again. Ask why doubling and doubling again has this effect. Give some examples:
$12 \times 4 = 12 \times 2 \times 2 = 48$
$8 \times 4 = 8 \times 2 \times 2 = 32$
Give examples of dividing by 4 or finding quarters by halving and halving again:
$60 \div 4$ or a quarter of $60 = 60 \div 2 \div 2 = 15$
$36 \div 4$ or a quarter of $36 = 36 \div 2 \div 2 = 9$

5. One-step problems

> **Objective:** Solve simple one-step word problems set in 'real life' contexts and explain how the problem was solved
> **Leading to:** Solving simple two-step word problems
> **Strand:** Solving problems
> **Topic:** 'Real life' problems

Group activity
Explaining methods and reasoning orally and writing a number sentence to show how the problem was solved.

Write a statement on the board and ask the children questions to do with it. Ask them to make up some questions of their own to ask you.

Example
A box holds 25 cakes.
How many cakes are left if you eat seven? How many cakes are left if you give away 18?
How many people can have five cakes each? How many cakes would there be in four boxes?
The larger sized box holds three times as many cakes. How many is that?
How many boxes are needed to hold 70 cakes?
Give the children statement cards similar to the idea above, with a few questions on for the children to answer and then ask them to make up their own set of questions to ask the class during the plenary session.

A spider has 8 legs.	A crate holds 36 cans of cola.
How many legs do 2 spiders have? Four? Eight? Sixteen? Bob had a collection of 10 spiders. How many legs? Sal has twice as many spiders as Bob. How many legs? How many spiders did Bob and Sal have together? Now make up some of your own questions.	12 cans a row, how many rows? The shop has 5 crates, how many cans? 19 cans were sold from one crate, how many left? Each can costs 55p. How much for 2 cans? Four? Eight? Sixteen? Thirty-two? How much for the whole crate? Now make up some of your own questions.

Plenary

Discuss the groups' problems. Choose one to work through some, a good example would be the cans of cola one. Pick some suitable questions, e.g. Each can costs 55p. How much for two cans? Four? Eight? Sixteen? Thirty-two? What is the best way to solve these? – doubling. How can we use that information to help us to work out how much the whole crate would cost? – add together the cost of 32 and four cans.

Tell the children that next time they will be solving similar problems, but those with two-steps. Give an example:

There are 25 books on the top shelf and twice as many on the bottom.

How many are there altogether?

How many more are on the bottom shelf?

Sue chose four books from the top shelf and12 from the bottom. *How many books were left?*

6. Measuring capacity

> **Objective:** Suggest suitable units to estimate or measure capacity
> **Leading to:** Reading scales with accuracy
> **Strand:** Measures
> **Topic:** Length, mass and capacity

Group activity

Collecting, displaying and labelling bottles holding from 50ml to 500ml of a liquid.

Show a litre bottle. Ask the children what types of liquid are usually measured in litres. Ask the children what smaller unit than a litre is often used to measure liquids. Find out if they know how many millilitres are equivalent to one litre. Ask what might be measured in millilitres. Show smaller containers, e.g. milkshake bottle, small pop bottle, cough mixture bottle, measuring jug.

Give the children some bottles of different sizes and a measuring jug. Ask them to accurately measure different amounts of water into each one and label. The amounts need to be multiples of 50, e.g. 50ml, 100ml, 150ml, 200ml, 250ml, 300ml, 350ml, 400ml, 450ml, 500ml or ½ litre.

Plenary

Ask one of the groups to show their work, by ordering the bottles from least amount of water to the greatest. Ask the group to describe how they measured the water accurately. Tell the children that, during their next lesson, they will be reading scales and measuring other amounts of water. Give a brief demonstration:

| How full is this jug? |

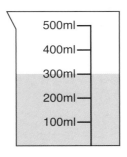

| I have 250ml in this jug and 550ml in this one. If I pour them both into here, what should the scale read? |

7. 2-D shapes

> **Objective:** Make shapes and patterns with increasing accuracy, and describe their features
> **Leading to:** Putting two or three identical shapes together to make a new one, naming the new shape and describing its features
> **Strand:** Shape and space
> **Topic:** Properties of 2-D shapes

Paired activity

Using 2-D shapes to make and describe pictures and patterns.

Demonstrate the paired activity using shapes either attached to a Velcro board or 'blutak' onto the board to make a picture or pattern.

Example

Describe the features of your picture or pattern:

> My pattern is made from a quadrilateral which is called a parallelogram, a triangle and a pentagon. It is repeated three times. There are no right angles in my pattern. There are 21 acute angles, 16 diagonal lines and several parallel lines.

Ask pairs of children to make up their own pictures or patterns. You could give the children a limit of three shapes to use or let them choose how many they want to use for themselves.

Plenary

Ask some of the pairs to show their patterns and describe them to the rest of the class.
Tell the children that during the next lesson they will be using one shape to make new shapes.

Examples

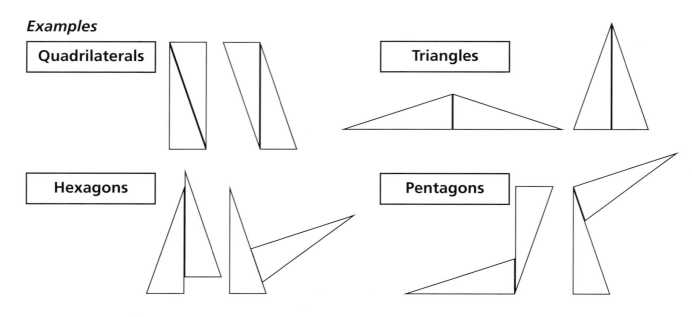

Quadrilaterals

Triangles

Hexagons

Pentagons

8. Position and direction

> **Objective:** Describe and find the position of a square on a grid
> **Leading to:** Describing directions using N, S, E and W
> **Strand:** Shape and space
> **Topic:** Position and direction

Paired activity

Finding positions on a grid with the rows and columns labelled; playing a game of 'Treasure Hunt'.

Demonstrate by drawing a grid on the board, similar to the one below. Ask some volunteers to colour in a square each. Ask the others to give the 'co-ordinates' to show where the coloured squares are, i.e. A5, C3, E2.

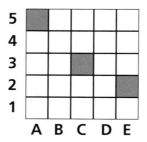

Give each pair of children similar grids, for the game of 'Treasure hunt'. One of the children colours a square and their partner has to guess where it is, giving the correct co-ordinates. Once their guess is correct, they 'hide' the treasure and the other partner guesses.

Plenary

Ask some of the class to feedback to the others.
Tell the children that as they have done so well, during the next lesson they will be making a plan and following directions using the terms N, S, E and W. Give a brief demonstration.

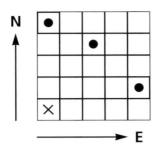

Collect the spots:
Start at x, move N 4, E 1,
S 2, E 3, S 1, W 2, N 2.

Year 4

9. Place value

Objective: Read and write whole numbers, know what each digit in a number represents
Leading to: Partitioning into thousands, hundreds, tens and units
Strand: Numbers and the number system
Topic: Place value

Paired activity

Finding cards to match numbers written in words.

Remind the children of the vocabulary associated with the number system and check to make sure they know how to spell the words, i.e. units or ones, tens, hundreds, thousands, ten thousands, hundred thousands, millions.
Give each pair of children two sets of cards, one with the numbers written in digits and the other in words. The children need to match them. See photocopiable sheet 8.

Plenary

Invite some of the pairs of children to come to the front of the class and show a few of their pairs of numbers. Ask them to hold them up and see if the rest of the class can read them. Tell the children that, because they have done so well, during the next lesson they will be using the written number cards and partitioning them, making up the number in digits. Give a quick example:

Four hundred and sixty four	400
	60
	4
	464

One hundred and ten thousand and sixteen	100 000
	10 000
	10
	6
	110 016

10. Multiplying and dividing

Objective: Multiply and divide whole numbers by 10
Leading to: Multiplying integers less than 1000 by 100
Strand: Numbers and the number system
Topic: Ordering (whole numbers)

Paired activity

Using multi-base equipment to multiply two-digit numbers by 10, then 10 again and again.

Demonstrate using multi-base as representations on an OHP with acetate labels:

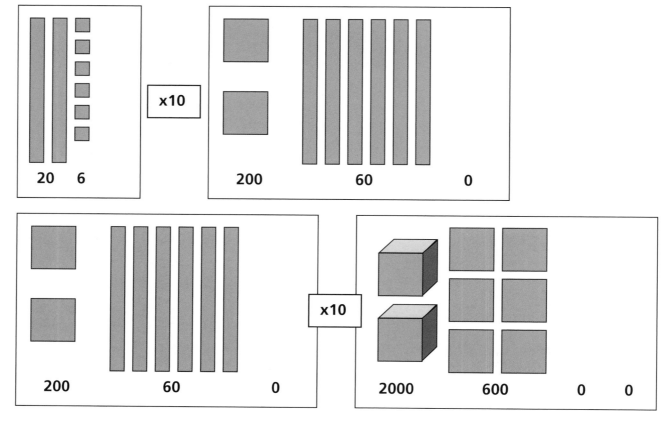

Once you have demonstrated using multi-base, use ordinary cubes, as they use up less space, are just as effective and can be used simply by the children during their paired work:

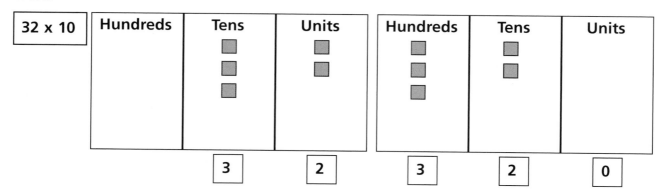

Ask the pairs to use their digit cards to create two-digit numbers. Ask them to draw them as above, multiply them by 10 and draw the result.

Plenary

Ask a few of the pairs to demonstrate their work. Ask the children to tell you what they think happens when they divide by 10. They should be able to tell you that the number gets 10 x smaller. Demonstrate this using one of the examples you began with:

320 ÷ 10	Hundreds	Tens	Units
	▪ ▪ ▪	▪ ▪	
	3	2	0

Hundreds	Tens	Units
	▪ ▪ ▪	▪ ▪
3	2

Tell the children that as they have achieved their objective for today, next time they will be looking at what happens when they multiply and divide numbers by 100. Put an example on the board and ask the children to predict:

Thousands	Hundreds	Tens	Units
		▪ ▪ ▪ ▪	▪▪ ▪▪ ▪▪ ▪▪
		4	8

Thousands	Hundreds	Tens	Units
	▪ ▪ ▪ ▪	▪▪ ▪▪ ▪▪ ▪▪	
4	8	0	0

11. Fractions and decimals

Objective: Use decimal notation, know what each digit in a decimal fraction represents
Leading to: Ordering sets of decimal numbers
Strand: Numbers and the number system
Topic: Fractions and decimals

Paired activity
Linking tenths as fractions to tenths as decimal fractions.

Demonstrate by working with fraction strips as shown below.

Example

Ask the children to tell you what fraction has been shaded, i.e. 3/10 or three tenths. Explain that another way of describing this would be to say that 0.3 has been shaded. Ask the children what mixed fraction has been shaded, i.e. 13/10 . Then ask them to tell you what decimal fraction this is, i.e.1.3.

Give the children a variety of strips similar to the ones above to convert to fractions and then equivalent decimal fractions.

Plenary
Invite the children to show and explain what they have been doing. Tell them that during the next lesson they will be learning to order different sets of decimal numbers on a number line. Give a brief demonstration:
Use a partially filled in number line. Write some of the missing numbers on cards and 'blutak' them to the board. Ask some of the children to find the correct space on the number line on to which to put them.

12. Mental doubling and halving

Objective: Use doubling and halving to multiply and divide by 4
Leading to: Use doubling and halving twice to multiply and divide by 8
Strand: Calculation
Topic: Mental calculation strategies (x and ÷)

Paired activity
Finding multiples of 4 by doubling and halving.

Discuss multiplying and dividing by 4 using doubling and halving. Ask the children when they think this method would be the most effective, i.e. when the numbers do not fall into the familiar part of the 4 times table. Demonstrate the paired activity:
Give the children a selection of two-digit cards. They need to write the number down and multiply and divide it by 4 whenever possible and record their answers.

Example

36	x 4 36, 72, <u>144</u>	÷ 4 36, 18, <u>9</u>
50	x 4 50, 100, <u>200</u>	÷ 4 50, 25, <u>12.5</u>
42	x 4 42, 84, <u>168</u>	÷ 4 42, 21, <u>10.5</u>

Plenary

Ask a few of the children to explain some of their calculations using the board. Tell the children that as they have worked so well on this objective, during the next lesson they will learn a quick way of multiplying and dividing by 8. Ask the children if they have any ideas. If they haven't, ask them about the relationship between 4 and 8 as a clue. Give a few examples:

4 x 8	4, 8, 16, 32	4 ÷ 8	4, 2, 1, 0.5
12 x 8	12, 24, 48, 96	12 ÷ 8	12, 6, 3, 1, 0.5
32 x 8	32, 64, 128, 256	32 ÷ 8	32, 16, 8, 4

13. Division

> **Objective:** Give a remainder as a whole number
> **Leading to:** Deciding what to do after division and round up or down accordingly
> **Strand:** Calculations
> **Topic:** Understanding division

Paired activity

Solving problems using division, by dividing using multiples of the divisor.

Examples

Remind the children of previous division work:

$$56 ÷ 4$$

$$
\begin{array}{ll}
56 & \\
\underline{40} & 10 \times 4 \\
16 & \\
\underline{16} & 4 \times 4 \\
0 &
\end{array}
$$

Answer: 14

Give the children some cards with problems on to work out, such as:

There are 64 children in Year 4.

How many teams of 6 children can be made?
How many children will be left over?

How many teams of 7 children can be made?
How many children will be left over?

How many teams of 8 children can be made?
How many children will be left over?

My friend had £20.

She shared it equally into 4 piles. How much in each pile?

She shared it equally into 8 piles. How much in each pile?

She shared it equally into 6 piles. How much in each pile and how much left?

Plenary

Choose one or two of the problem cards to work through with the children. Tell them that during their next lesson they will need to round their answers up or down according to what the problem is asking. Give an example adapted from the problems used in this lesson: There are 64 children in Year 4. They are going on an outing in some coaches. Each coach will carry 30 children: how many coaches will they need?

14. Measuring

> **Objective:** Estimate and measure lengths with increasing accuracy to the nearest centimetre
> **Leading to:** Estimating and measuring accurately to the nearest half centimetre.
> **Strand:** Measures
> **Topic:** Length, mass and capacity

Group activity

Making worms and estimating and measuring their lengths.

Remind the children of their past work on length, revise the number of centimetres in a metre, metres in a kilometre and millimetres in a centimetre. Demonstrate the group activity: Give each child a lump of plasticine. Each child needs to use it to make five worms of different lengths. They then need to order their worms from shortest to longest, estimate and then measure their lengths to the nearest centimetre and work out how close their estimate was to the real length. Record in a table similar to the one below:

	Estimated length	Actual length	Difference
Worm 1			
Worm 2			
Worm 3			
Worm 4			
Worm 5			

Ask each member of the group to then choose their shortest and longest worms and order them amongst the shortest and longest from the rest of their group members.

Plenary

Discuss the work carried out in the lesson. Find out if the children's estimating skills improved the more they practised. Ask each group to choose two worms and bring them to the front. As a class, order, estimate and measure them.
Tell the children that during the next lesson they will be doing something similar, but measuring to the nearest half centimetre. Give a quick example using five lengths of wool or string.

15. Perimeter

> **Objective: Measure and calculate the perimeter of simple shapes**
> **Leading to:** Finding a short way to work out the perimeter of squares and rectangles
> **Strand:** Measures
> **Topic:** Area and perimeter

Paired activity

Drawing different sized rectangles and squares and measuring their perimeters.

Remind the children what the perimeter of a shape is. Demonstrate how to find the perimeter using a transparent ruler and a square cut from card on an OHP.
Give pairs of children different sized squares and rectangles and ask them to find their perimeters. They could record by drawing around each shape and writing an addition sum.

Plenary

Discuss the work that the children have been doing. Ask them if anyone can think of a quick way of calculating the perimeter that doesn't involve adding all the numbers, i.e:
Rectangle: double 6cm + double 4cm instead of 6cm + 6cm + 4cm + 4cm.
Square: 6cm x 4 instead of 6cm + 6cm + 6cm + 6cm.
Tell the children that during the next lesson they will be using this method to work out more complicated perimeters made by putting two squares or rectangles together, e.g.

Example

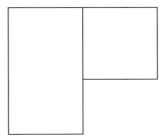

16. Using co-ordinates

> **Objective:** Recognise positions and directions, and use co-ordinates
> **Leading to:** Using the eight compass directions N, S, E, W, NE, NW, SE, SW
> **Strand:** Shape and space
> **Topic:** Position and direction

Paired activity

Following directions along a grid using the directions N, S, E, W and numbers to find points previously plotted with co-ordinates.

Demonstrate plotting crosses on a grid using co-ordinates, then give a grid to each child and ask them to plot crosses on the co-ordinates that you call out. See the example below, and use photocopiable sheet 9 for a blank 5 x 5 grid.

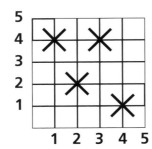

Can you see where I've plotted my crosses?

They are at (1,4) (2,2) (3,4) (4,1)

Ask the children to plot crosses on their blank 5 X 5 grid of the following co-ordinates: (2, 5) (1, 2) (2, 3) and (5, 4).

Ask the children to play a tracking game in pairs: Give them two large blank grids (see photocopiable sheet 9) 10 squares by 10 . Ask one of the children to plot six crosses on their grid and then direct their partner to where their crosses are, using the compass directions N, S, E and W. Their partner needs to make a duplicate copy of the grid from the instructions that they have been given.

Plenary

Ask a couple of the children to try their instructions out on the rest of the class. Discuss what was easy or difficult about the activity. Tell the children that next time they will be learning about the directions NE, NW, SE and SW. Ask the children what they think these directions might be.

Photocopiable Sheet 6
Digit cards

1	2	3
4	5	6
7	8	9
0	0	0

Photocopiable Sheet 7
The Halving Game

Photocopiable Sheet 8

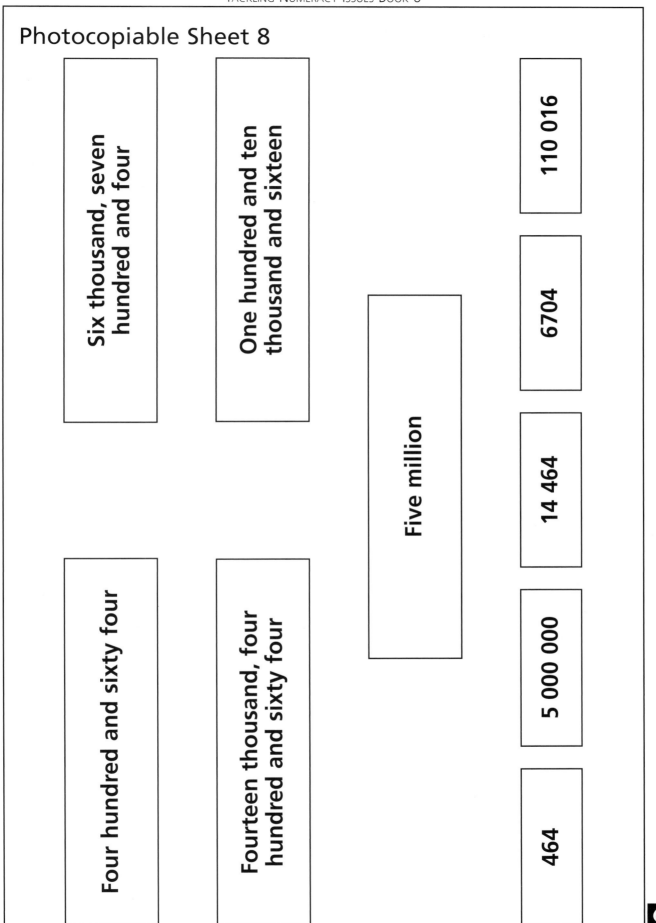

Six thousand, seven hundred and four

One hundred and ten thousand and sixteen

Four hundred and sixty four

Fourteen thousand, four hundred and sixty four

Five million

110 016

6704

14 464

5 000 000

464

Photocopiable Sheet 9

Chapter 3
Links to other maths topics and curriculum areas

The Framework for Teaching Mathematics has a very helpful section on making links between the subjects. It states that 'you need to look for opportunities for drawing mathematical experience out of a wide range of children's activities.'
Maths contributes to many subjects in the primary curriculum, often in practical ways, and these links often help to validate the purposes of maths.
Maths and other areas of curriculum subjects can complement each other. It is important that links are made as it helps the children to see the relevance of what they are learning in the overall picture of their education. It is often too easy to treat the curriculum subjects as isolated areas that must be covered. Linking makes it all the more real to the children as it can put what they are learning into contexts they can appreciate.

Subject links (extracts from the NNS Framework):

English: Maths lessons can help develop and support pupils' literacy skills by teaching mathematical vocabulary and technical terms, asking children to read and interpret problems to identify the mathematical content, and by encouraging them to explain, argue and present conclusions to others.
Science: Almost every scientific investigation or experiment is likely to require one or more of the mathematical skills of classifying, counting, measuring, calculating, estimating and recording in tables and graphs.
Art, D & T: Measurements are often needed in art and design and technology. Many patterns and constructions are based on spatial ideas and properties of shapes including symmetry.
ICT: Children will apply and use mathematics in a variety of ways when they solve problems using ICT. For example, they will collect and classify data, enter it into data-handling software, produce graphs and tables, and interpret and explain their results.
History, geography and RE: In various circumstances children will collect data by counting and measuring, use co-ordinates, ideas of angle, direction, position, scale and ratio. Patterns of days of the week, the calendar, annual festivals and passages of time all have a mathematical basis.
PE and music: These often require measurement of height, distance and time, counting, symmetry, movement, position and direction.

Plenary sessions can be used to discuss work carried out in the objectives taught and linked to work that has been or will be studied in subjects such those mentioned.

This chapter is designed to show where some of the possible links are, in order to get you thinking about making links in literacy, science, history, geography, art and PE, as well as other maths topics.

Literacy

Links between numeracy and literacy are plentiful.

In the Curriculum Guidelines for English, it states that children should be taught to:

- ✪ Speak clearly, fluently and confidently to different people;
- ✪ Listen, understand and respond to others;
- ✪ Join as members of a group;
- ✪ Participate in a range of drama activities;
- ✪ Be part of group discussion and interaction;
- ✪ Be taught grammatical constructions that are characteristic of spoken standard English and how language varies.

In maths all of these are encouraged as a matter of course by, for example:

- ✪ Explaining strategies to others;
- ✪ Listening to and discussing other children's methods of working out calculations;
- ✪ Working on activities in a group;
- ✪ Imagining and acting out problems in the problem-solving strand;
- ✪ Discussing and interacting with each other in group work;
- ✪ Learning, understanding and using new vocabulary.

Year 3

1. Mental addition

> **Objective:** Add mentally three or more numbers, within a range of 1 to about 50
> **Strand:** Calculations
> **Topic:** Understanding addition

Possible activities

Give each pair of children a selection of about 15 cards with a number between 1 and 20 written on each. See the number card sheets at the back of the book. Ask them to place the cards in a pile face down in front of them. Give them a time limit and ask them to pick five cards and total the digits. How many sets of five cards can they total in the time allowed? Call out several numbers; ask the children to add them mentally and write down their answer on a piece of paper.

Write some numbers on the board, give the children a minute to total them and show their answer using digit cards. There are digit cards on photocopiable sheet 6.

Plenary

During the plenary, display a coding card with letters of the alphabet and numbers, e.g. A = 1, B = 2, C = 3, D = 4, E = 5, F = 6 etc. See photocopiable sheet 10. Write on the board some words that rhyme with each other, e.g. fright, bright, might. Ask the children to find the value of these words, i.e. fright = 6 + 18 + 9 + 7 + 8 + 20 = 68. Ask – "Is there a quick way to find the total of these particular words?" Someone should be able to tell you that if you work out the value of the 'ight', then you just need to add on the other letters each time.

Then tell the children that during their next literacy lesson, they will be working with words similar to the ones that they have used during this plenary session and totalling their values.

2. 2-D shape vocabulary

> **Objective:** Use, read and begin to write the vocabulary from the previous year and extend to pentagonal, hexagonal, octagonal
> **Strand:** Shape and space
> **Topic:** Properties of 2-D shapes

Possible activities

Concentrate on the vocabulary of the following shapes: circular, triangular, rectangular, pentagonal, hexagonal, octagonal. Give the children a variety of shapes and ask them to sort them according to the criteria indicated by the vocabulary.

Hide a shape and slowly reveal it, asking the children what they think the shape is and why. Describe a variety of shapes and ask the children to draw them and label them with the appropriate adjective from the vocabulary for the lesson.

Plenary

During the plenary revise the vocabulary of the lesson. Ask some children to draw on the board an octagonal shape, a rectangular shape and so on. Have prepared the vocabulary on pieces of card and ask other children to label the shapes that have been drawn.

Tell the children that this work will help them in their next literacy lesson when they will be making up a glossary or sentences using these words.

3. Units of time

> **Objective:** Know and use units of time and the relationships between them
> **Strand:** Measures
> **Topic:** Time

Possible activities

Give groups of children some cards to match and ask them to record their answers.

Examples

1 hour	1 day	1 week	60 seconds	1 year

24 hours	60 minutes	365 days	1 minute	7 days

Give the children the page of a calendar that has the 12 months and their dates on. Ask them to find out how many days there are in each month. Ask them to find out how many weekends there are in each month. Ask them if they think their answer will be the same in another year and investigate whether their answer is correct.

Plenary
Ask the children to feed back to the rest of the class, the work that they have been doing. Then ask the children to choose a special day during the year (other than their birthday!) to describe to the other children. Tell the children that during their next literacy lesson they will be writing about their important day.

4.'Real life' problems

> **Objective:** Use own mental strategies to solve simple story problems set in real life
> **Strand:** Solving problems
> **Topic:** 'Real life' problems

Possible activity
Ask the children to work in groups of three or four. Give them a card with a problem on. They need to work out a short play to describe their problem, which they will 'act out' to their peers. Give the children paper, pens and other apparatus that they can use to help them with their scenario.

Problem suggestions

Sam had three packs of stickers. He gave 12 stickers away and had 18 left.
How many stickers were in each pack?

There were 34 books in the library. Sue borrowed five, Jane six, Paul nine and Tom two.
How many were left?

John had £26. He shared it equally between himself and his three friends.
How much did they each have?

There were four tomato plants in the garden. Each plant grew three tomatoes.
How many tomatoes were there altogether?

Ben had four pairs of shoes.
He lost one shoe while he was at school.
How many shoes did he have left?

Sam, Adam, Jenny, Peter and Jane had a picnic.
Peter brought 20 biscuits to share equally with his friends.
How many will they each have?

There were three sunflower plants in the garden.
One grew to a height of 2m, the second to half that
height and the third to half that height.
How tall was the smallest sunflower?

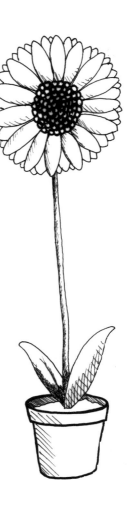

Tommy and her friends went to the shop.
They bought a loaf of bread for 60p and some milk for 45p.
They gave the shopkeeper £5.
How much change did they receive?

My dad drove us to the seaside for a weekend break.
It took us 2 hours and 15 minutes to get there. We left at 9am.
What time did we arrive?

Plenary
Select one or two of the groups of children to act out their 'scene' to the rest of the class.
The class need to work out what is happening in the 'scene' and the answer to the problem.

Tell the children that during their next literacy lesson, they will be using the scenes they
made up during this lesson to concentrate on, using character, action and narrative to
convey their problem.

Year 4

1. Ordering numbers

> **Objective:** Ordering a set of numbers
> **Strand:** Numbers and the number system
> **Topic:** Ordering

Possible activities
Give the children some cards with four-digit whole numbers written on, the first three digits
of each being the same. Ask the children to order the cards from smallest to greatest and
then record.

Put some four-digit numbers on the board. Ask the children to draw a number line each
and plot the numbers onto the line in the correct order.

Plenary

Write some random numbers on the board, making sure some begin with the same three digits. Ask the children to help order them, explaining what their thought processes are as they go along.

Finish the plenary by explaining to the children that not only is ordering important in maths it is also important in literacy. Put some examples of words on the board (mathematical if possible) that begin with the same three or four letters, e.g. pentagon, perimeter. Ask the children how they would order them alphabetically. Ask them why this knowledge is important; encourage an answer such as: "So we can look it up in the dictionary to find its meaning". Tell the children that during their next literacy lesson they will be ordering words, just as they have been ordering numbers today.

2. 3-D and 2-D shapes

> **Objective:** Classify 3-D shapes according to their properties
> **Strand:** Shape and space
> **Topic:** Properties of 3-D and 2-D shapes

Possible activities

Make a collection of shapes that are polyhedrons by identifying the following properties: each face is flat and is a polygon; an edge is a straight line where two edges meet; a vertex is the point where three or more edges meet.
Make a Carroll diagram to sort a variety of 3-D shapes.

Example

	More than one square face	More than one triangular face	
Five or less edges			**Draw the misfits here!**
Six or more edges			

Plenary

Ask some groups of children to show their Carroll diagrams and explain how they decided where each shape should go. Ask the children to tell you what the 'properties' rule is for polyhedral shapes.

Invite some children to think of some ways in which they might find it easy to remember these properties. Then tell them that during their next literacy lesson they will be making up rhyming jingles about the properties of 3-D shapes.

3. Solving problems

Objective: Use all four operations to solve word problems involving numbers in 'real life'
Strand: Solving problems
Topic: 'Real life' problems

Possible activity

Discuss the things the children need to think about when they see a word problem:

- ✪ What is the question asking us?
- ✪ What information do we have that will help us?
- ✪ What do we need to find out?
- ✪ How can we find it out?
- ✪ What is a good estimate of the answer?
- ✪ Does our actual answer seem sensible?
- ✪ How does it compare with our estimate?

Put an example on acetate on the OHP and work through it.

Put some numbers on the board, e.g.

| 250, 100, 75 |
| £20, £25, £3.50 |
| 12m, 2.5m, 30cms |

Ask the children to work in pairs to make up some interesting problems using those numbers. Specify the operations you want each pair to use for differentiation purposes.

Plenary

Choose some pairs of children to tell the class their problems. Work through the problems, asking the questions above.

Tell the children that during their next literacy lesson they will be listening to the other problems that the rest of the class made up. They will be thinking about gaining and maintaining the interest and responses of the other children by making their problems more interesting.

4. 2-D and 3-D shape vocabulary

Objective: Describe 3-D and 2-D shapes using the adjectives circular, triangular, rectangular, pentagonal, hexagonal, octagonal, spherical, cylindrical
Strand: Shape and space
Topic: Properties of 3-D and 2-D shapes

Possible activities

Sort a selection of 2-D shapes according to the adjectives in the lesson objective.

Draw some repeating patterns using shapes that are triangular, circular or rectangular. Identify octagonal shapes from a selection drawn on paper.

Draw as many different pentagonal and hexagonal shapes as possible on squared paper.

Plenary

Invite some children to show their patterns or shape drawings. Expect them to describe them using the correct vocabulary.

Ask the children to tell you why a shape is called circular, triangular etc. They should be able to refer to the root word, which in each case is the noun. List the relevant words on the board:

Noun	Adjective
Circle	Circular
Triangle	Triangular
Rectangle	Rectangular
Pentagon	Pentagonal
Hexagon	Hexagonal
Heptagon	Heptagonal
Octagon	Octagonal

Tell the children that during their next literacy lesson they will be looking at other nouns and the suffixes that change them into adjectives.

Science

Links between numeracy and science are plentiful. They mostly come under the strand of Handling data, although working with numbers and measures obviously plays an important part.

In the Curriculum Guidelines for Science, it states that children should be taught to:

✪ Ask questions that can be investigated scientifically and decide how they might find answers to them;
✪ Think about what might happen or try things out before deciding what to do;
✪ Check observations and measurements by repeating them where appropriate;
✪ Use a wide range of methods, including diagrams, drawings, tables, bar charts, line graphs and ICT, to communicate data in an appropriate and systematic manner;
✪ Make comparisons and identify simple patterns or associations in their own observations and measurements or other data;
✪ Review their work and the work of others and describe its significance and limitations.

In maths all of these are encouraged in different ways, for example:

✪ Asking questions such as: "Which is the best way to answer this calculation?"; "What would happen if I did it this way?"; "What do I need to know to solve this problem?"
✪ Estimating answers;
✪ Recording measurements with length, mass, capacity and time;
✪ Solving a problem by collecting, representing and interpreting data;
✪ Making comparisons and identifying patterns in number, shapes and measures;
✪ Checking and explaining strategies, deciding on the efficiency of their methods.

The Handling data strand is probably the best way to link the two subjects.
There are five aspects of data handling in numeracy that need to be considered:

✪ Specifying the problem – formulating questions in terms of the data that is needed and the type of inferences that can be made from them.
✪ Planning – deciding what data needs collecting, including sample size and data format and what statistical analysis needs to be carried out.
✪ Collecting data – from a variety of appropriate sources including experiments, surveys and primary and secondary data.
✪ Processing and representing – including lists, tables and charts.
✪ Interpreting and discussion – relating the summarised data to the initial question.

It is often appropriate to use a problem that needs solving in science to satisfy these requirements. The interpreting and discussing aspect can be achieved during the plenary session and then taken into the science lesson to use as needed.

This part of the chapter concentrates on possible problems that can be solved in numeracy and then taken into the science lesson.

Year 3

1. Teeth and eating

> **Objectives:**
> To turn ideas about the diet of animals into a form that can be investigated
> To decide how many animals should be investigated and the range of foods to be considered
> To present evidence about the foods eaten by animals in a suitable bar chart or pictogram
> To decide whether the evidence is sufficient to draw conclusions

Possible science activity
Decide as a class on one question to investigate, e.g. Do all cats eat the same food?
Discuss what evidence to collect, e.g. which cats should be included, and how to describe different sorts of food (fish, chicken, tinned food).

Numeracy: Handling data lesson
Remind the children of the problem that is being investigated in their science lesson.
Help children to decide how to collect and present the evidence, e.g. tables, pictograms or bar charts.

Give the children some time during the lesson to actually present their evidence as decided.

Plenary

Talk with the children about how good the evidence is, e.g. how many pets there were in the sample.

Decide what, if any, conclusions can be drawn.

Take this conclusion back to the next science lesson.

2. Growth of plants

Objectives:
To make careful observations and measurements of plants growing
To use simple apparatus to measure the height of plants in standard measures
To use results to draw conclusions
To decide that plants need leaves to grow well

Possible science activity

Introduce the idea of a plant as an organism in which different parts, e.g. leaf, stem and root, all need to work properly if the plant is to grow well.
Present the children with two similar plants of the same species, such as geranium, and ask them to suggest how these could be used to find out whether plants need leaves to grow well.

Respond to the children's suggestions or remove many of the leaves from one plant; keep both in the same place and water equally.

Discuss with the children what they are going to measure and observe, e.g. height from soil level to the tip of the shoot, colour and number of leaves.

Over a period of several weeks, help each child to make and record careful measurements of the height of the plants.

Numeracy: Handling data lesson

Remind the class of the work they have been doing in science over the last few weeks and tell them that today they are going to bring it to a conclusion.

Using the measurement records that each child has made, ask each one to work on their own or with a friend to make a bar chart to represent their findings. Suggest that the vertical axis should represent the heights of the two plants, and the horizontal, the days that they were measured on. Other than that guidance, give them a free hand to represent their results as they wish.

Plenary

Invite some of the children to explain their bar charts to the rest of the class. Discuss as a whole class, whether the charts are all similar. Did anyone produce something different?

Talk with children about what the results show.

What conclusion can they come to in answer to the original question – 'Do plants need leaves to grow well?'

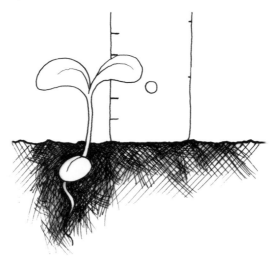

Year 4

3. Moving and growing

> **Objectives:**
> To identify a question and turn it into a form that can be tested making a prediction
> To decide precisely what body measurement to make and to make it
> To use bar charts or pictograms to present measurements
> To say what the evidence shows and whether it supports the prediction

Possible science activity

Ask the children to suggest ideas about differences and help them turn them into a form that can be investigated, e.g.

- ✪ Who has the longer arms – children or adults, boys or girls?
- ✪ Are adults' heads bigger than children's heads?
- ✪ I think Year 6 children have longer arms than Year 4 children.

Discuss with the children exactly how they make their measurements in order to make reliable comparisons and how they will present their results, e.g. by making tables, bar charts or pictograms of the two categories.

Numeracy: Handling data lesson
Remind the children what they are intending to investigate.

In groups, ask the children to take the measurements they need to make, for example of adults' heads and children's heads according to the discussions carried out in science about making reliable comparisons.

After making the measurements, ask them to display their results on a bar chart.

Plenary
Talk with the children about the bar charts, asking them to describe what they show. Can they come to a conclusion to take back to their next science lesson?

4. Habitats

> **Objectives:**
> To find out that different animals are found in different habitats
> To make predictions of organisms that will be found in a habitat
> To observe the conditions in a local habitat and make a record of the animals found
> To conclude that animals are suited to the environment in which they are found

Possible science activity
Using pictures of places in the immediate locality or similar to those in the locality as stimuli, ask the children to predict where a particular organism will be found, e.g. woodlice, snail, butterfly, bee.

Visit a locality to check the children's predictions.

Explain that collecting animals must be done with care so that the animals are not damaged. Help the children to collect invertebrates and record the locations in which they were found.

Ask the children to observe and describe the conditions, e.g. light, water, soil, shade, temperature.

Ask the children whether they found the organisms they expected.
Help the children to return any animals collected to their habitat.

Numeracy: Handling data lesson:
Discuss with the children the location of the animals they observed during their science lesson. Tell them that they now need to record their information on a bar chart or pictogram. Give them the choice.

Expect the children to complete their representation by the end of the lesson.

Plenary
During the plenary, ask the children to discuss their findings according to their representations. What can they conclude?

History

Links between numeracy and history are evident in the strands of Calculations and Solving problems.

In the Curriculum Guidelines for History, it states that children should be taught to:

✪ Place events, people and changes into correct periods of time;
✪ Use dates and vocabulary relating to the passing of time.

In maths, this Attainment Target can be supported during the teaching of different topics, for example:

✪ Number operations and the relationship between them;
✪ Developing rapid recall of number facts;
✪ Developing a range of mental strategies for finding, from known facts, those that they cannot recall;
✪ Carrying out simple calculations;
✪ Choose sensible calculation methods to solve whole-number problems.

Years 3 and 4

For both of the following units use a similar number line activity and plenary as shown below.

1. Unit 6A: Why have people invaded and settled in Britain in the past? A Roman case study

Who were the Celts and who were the Romans?

> **Objectives:**
> To select and record information about Celtic and Roman ways of life
> To make comparisons between these lifestyles
> To understand about aspects of Celtic and Roman Britain, using a variety of resources

Possible activities

Ask the children to locate the Roman period on the class time line. Tell them that they are going to find out about the Romans and also about the Celts, who lived in Britain before the Romans arrived.

Give them information about and pictures of the Celts and/or the Romans. Ask the children to complete a three-column grid with the headings: 'How they did things', 'Celts', and 'Romans'. In the first column children can list aspects such as dress, belief, language, towns, farms, art, technology. They can use the other two columns to compare the two ways of life.

Discuss the children's answers with them, drawing their attention to similarities and differences.

2. Unit 6A: Why have people invaded and settled in Britain in the past? An Anglo-Saxon case study

How was the grave at Sutton Hoo discovered?

> **Objectives:**
> To locate the Anglo-Saxon period on a time line
> To find out what was discovered at Sutton Hoo
> To know what we can and cannot learn from objects
> To make inferences from archaeological evidence

Possible activities

Tell the children that they will find out about an event from the time the Anglo-Saxons settled in Britain. Ask them to locate the Anglo-Saxon period on the class time line. Tell the children about the discovery of the ship burial at Sutton Hoo, the story of the mounds, where they were discovered and about the group of archaeologists who investigated the site.

Ask the children what they know about archaeology. Build on this to provide a brief overview of what an archaeologist does and why.

Possible numeracy activity

During a lesson on ordering numbers, give the children a number line or ask them to draw one and plot on it these numbers:

$$-2000 \qquad -1000 \qquad 0 \qquad 1000 \qquad 2000$$

The negative numbers represent BC times. Give the children various dates including the time of the Celts and the Romans or the Anglo-Saxons or all three and ask them to plot them onto their 'historical' number line.

Plenary

During the plenary session, remind the children of what they have been studying in history and ask them what their historical number line shows and why it is a helpful representation of the dates you have given them.

Bring in some mental calculation by asking the children to work out how many years there are between various times on their lines and for how long these periods in history lasted.

Tell them that they will be using this information to make a class time line in their next history lesson.

Geography

Links between numeracy and geography are obvious when looking at the strand Shape and space within the topics of Position and direction and Movement and angle. Various aspects can be incorporated into Handling data.

In the Curriculum Guidelines for Geography, it states that children should be taught to:

- Collect and record evidence, e.g. by carrying out a survey of shop functions and showing them on a graph;
- Communicate in ways appropriate to the task and audience;
- Use appropriate geographical vocabulary, e.g. temperature, transport industry;
- Use atlases and globes, maps and plans at a range of scales, e.g. using contents, keys and grids;
- Draw maps and plans at a range of scales, e.g. a sketch map of a locality

In maths all of these are encouraged in different ways, for example:

- Solve a relevant problem by collecting, organising, representing, extracting and interpreting data in tables, graphs and charts;
- Use the correct language, symbols and vocabulary associated with number and data;
- Communicate in spoken, pictorial and written form, using mathematical language and symbols;
- Present results in an organised way;
- Recognise positions and directions, and use co-ordinates;
- Use the eight compass directions N, S, E, W, NE, NW, SE, SW.

Year 3

1. Unit 6: Investigating our local area

> **Objectives:**
> To investigate places
> To learn about the wider context places
> To make maps and plans
> To use and interpret maps

Possible geography idea
Where is the locality in relation to other places? Where is our school?

Ask the children to locate on a globe and then, on progressively larger scale maps, a region, county, village.

Ask the children to find the school site on a map and aerial photographs of the village. Ask them to give directions from the school to specific points in the village, recording their directions on a map and identifying features in sequence.

Possible numeracy lesson idea

Remind the children about the work that they are doing in geography. Prepare a map/plan of a theme park or treasure island with co-ordinate lines on but no labels. Display this map/plan and ask some volunteers to label it with letters and numbers using pre-prepared 'post-it' notes. Discuss where to find various places/objects using the co-ordinates. You could follow this up with group, paired or individual work, e.g. finding the quickest way to get from one place to another; finding as many ways as possible to get from one end of the map to the other without entering a square that has a place/object in it. Either in this lesson or the next, move on to atlas work. Ask the children to look at a map of the UK and tell you the co-ordinates for various cities and tell you what town is near a co-ordinate that you call out.

Plenary

Look at the atlas again. This time find a co-ordinate for a city, e.g. London, and bring in the directions N, S, E, W, NE, NW, SE, SW. Which is the first town you come to if you go N of London? SE of London? etc.

Tell the children that during their next geography lesson they will be using the skills from today's numeracy lesson to help them to follow directions on a map, record where they are and identify features that they pass.

Year 4

2. Unit 8: What is the environment like in school?

> **Objectives:**
> To ask and respond to geographical questions
> To collect and record evidence to answer questions
> To understand how people affect the environment

Possible geography idea

What do we throw away in the classroom? How could it be reduced?

At the end of each day for a week, collect all the classroom rubbish, estimate how much there is and weigh it.

Ask the children to produce a cumulative graph for an interactive display, that shows the weight of rubbish throughout the week. Arrange for a small group to sort the rubbish into different types and produce a tally chart to add to the display.
Discuss with the children which types might be recycled and how to go about it, e.g. using bottle banks, newspaper collection, compost heaps, jumble sales, aluminium collection.
Discuss with the children why recycling is important.

> **N.B.**
> **Please ensure that there are no unsafe materials in the classroom rubbish, and that children wear rubber gloves.**

Possible numeracy lesson idea

The first two ideas from above would make an ideal basis for a series of lessons during the Measures topic in the Framework. The collection can be made at the end of each day and worked with during the following day's numeracy lesson. Allow the children to work in groups and estimate and weigh one part of the classroom rubbish each day. They will then need to sort their rubbish into different types and make tally charts. Each day they could add all their information to a class display.

Plenary

Discuss the children's findings each day. At the end of the week draw together all that has been discovered, with a particular emphasis on the tallies of types of rubbish. This record will then be taken to their geography lesson, where they will be considering recycling.

Art

Links between numeracy and art are evident in the strand of Shape and space.

In the Curriculum Guidelines for Art, it states that children:

✪ Should be taught about visual and tactile elements, including colour, pattern and texture, line and tone, shape, form and space, and how these elements can be combined and organised for different purposes;
✪ Should work on their own, and collaborate with others, on projects in two and three dimensions and on different scales.

In maths, these Attainment Targets can be supported during the teaching of different topics, for example:

✪ Describing properties of shapes that they can see or visualise using the related vocabulary;
✪ Creating 2-D shapes and 3-D shapes;
✪ Recognising reflective symmetry, rotations and translations in familiar 2-D shapes and patterns.

Years 3 and 4

1. Unit 3B: Investigating pattern

The following art and design activity would be ideal for a numeracy lesson on reflective symmetry, reflection and translation.

Ask the children to cut out multiple copies of a simple paper shape. Then ask them to arrange the shape in different patterns, using a grid to ensure the pattern they make is repeated regularly.

Encourage the children to use their knowledge and understanding of maths to create different patterns, e.g. by rotating, reflecting, translating in different positions.

Plenary
Ask the children to describe their patterns to their neighbours and invite some to describe theirs to the whole class.

Tell the children that they will be using their work from this numeracy lesson in their next art and design session when they will be cutting out a second shape, thinking about its relationship to the first – Will it be smaller or larger? Will it be a contrasting shape, size and colour? How will it be positioned in relation to the first shape? Will it overlap, be set inside or fit in a space between? They will add it to their original pattern.

Other possible numeracy lesson ideas
Talk about shapes and patterns in leaves.

Talk about the shapes in curtains, clothes, materials.

Design patterns using the 2-D shapes relevant to their year group.

Make halves of paper shapes by folding and make them into symmetrical patterns.

Combine four squares to make new shapes.

Use pinboards and elastic bands to make irregular pentagons and hexagons.

Make, talk about and describe symmetrical patterns made by ink blots or paint.

Plenaries
At the beginning of each plenary tell the children of the links you are making with their artwork. Show suitable pictures or artefacts to illustrate what these links are. Look at the children's work and compare to the artwork that is relevant. Tell the children what they will be doing in art as a result of their numeracy work.

PE

Links between numeracy and PE are evident in the strand of Shape and space, in the topics Position and direction and movement and angle.

In the Curriculum Guidelines for PE, it states that children should be taught to:

✪ Create and perform dances, using a range of movement patterns, including those from different times, places and cultures;
✪ Respond to a range of stimuli and accompaniment;
✪ Create and perform fluent sequences on the floor and using apparatus;
✪ Include variations in level, speed and direction in their sequences.

Years 3 and 4

In the Framework for teaching Mathematics, it is suggested that work covered in the following parts of the numeracy lesson can be reinforced during PE:

✪ Follow and give instructions to move in particular directions, e.g. face west, turn clockwise through one right angle;
✪ Know that after turning through half a turn, or two quarter turns in the same direction, you will be facing the opposite direction.

These Year 3 objectives can be extended to Year 4 objectives and reinforced in PE.

During plenary sessions make reference to the fact that you will be following up certain activities physically in PE.

Other areas of maths

During plenary sessions for work on Numbers and the number system make links to measures and money, e.g. ask questions relating the numbers to:

Money: 'I have £3.75; Sue has £3.15. Who has the most and by how much?'

Length: 'My Mum has 6m of string. She used 75cms to wrap up a parcel. How much did she have left?'

Weight: I needed 1kg of flour to bake my bread. I had 300g. How much more did I need?'

Capacity: 'I drank one 500ml bottle of coke. My friend drank 4 bottles. How many litres of coke did he drink?'

Time: 'If there are 60 minutes in one hour, how many are there in 4½ hours?'

Including aspects of data handling during plenaries related to other topics in maths is a useful way of reinforcing work done previously in this topic. It provides a useful link and enhances the relevance of data handling in general.

Draw some tables or charts on the board and put information on them that is relevant to the objective you have been teaching. For example:

A Carroll diagram to record multiples of 5 up to 50

Even	Not even
10	5
20	15
30	25
40	35
50	45

A Venn diagram to record a selection of 2-digit number cards

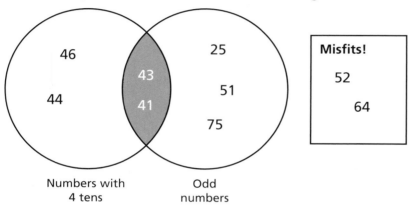

A Carroll diagram for sorting shapes

	No lines of symmetry	At least one line of symmetry
4 sides or more		
3 sides or more		

Put the work you have been doing into a real-life problem context, by visualising, asking the children to make up a problem or asking the children one of your own. This will be covered more thoroughly in the next chapter.

These three methods will reinforce the relevance of the maths that they have been learning.

Photocopiable Sheet 10
Code chart

A	B	C	D	E	F	G	H	I	J
1	2	3	4	5	6	7	8	9	10

K	L	M	N	O	P	Q	R	S	T
11	12	13	14	15	16	17	18	19	20

U	V	W	X	Y	Z
21	22	23	24	25	26

Chapter 4
Problem solving and games

Using and applying the skills that the children have been taught is one of the most important elements of numeracy. Ideas need to be put into context for the children so they can see the sense and relevance of what they have learnt. Many children have difficulty with problem-solving activities; so it is vital to provide them with lots of short sessions in which to practise these skills. The plenary part of the lesson can help, as it is an opportunity to put what they have been learning into a 'real life' situation.

After lessons from the strands of Numbers and the number system, Calculations, involving addition, subtraction and mental calculation strategies, incorporate some of the ideas below within your plenaries to help put the more abstract number work into context:

Visualising

Children often find visualising difficult and need to practise this skill. If they can see a word problem in their minds it will be easier for them to relate to it and therefore understand it and come up with a solution. It is also a useful way of introducing the vocabulary associated with problem solving, e.g. How many more? How many altogether? What is the difference?

You may need to alter the numbers depending on the age and ability of the children.

1. Close your eyes. Imagine you are holding a frying pan. It has a pancake in it. You are tossing the pancake. Now you are putting it on a plate. Now you are tossing another one and putting it on the plate. Now do the same with six more.
   How many pancakes are on your plate now?
   You are going to eat half of them.
   How many are left?

2. Imagine you have tossed ten pancakes and put them on the plate. Now you are going to toss seven more.
   How many have you got altogether?

3. Imagine you have tossed 21 pancakes. You are going to share them equally between yourself and your two friends.
   How many will be left?

4. Ben has three goldfish. They love to swim around in their bowl. Imagine the goldfish in their bowl. Can you see them? They blow big bubbles. Each fish blows six bubbles.
   How many bubbles are there?

5. *If each fish blows six bubbles and there are 60 bubbles, how many fish are there?*

6. Close your eyes and imagine ten bubbles, two for each fish.
   How many fish do you need for all the bubbles?

7. Sam and Carol both like cherries. Carol has some cherries for her lunch; she is going to share them equally with Sam. She has eight cherries.
   How many will they have each?
   Close your eyes and imagine Sam and Carol eating their lunch. Imagine Carol sharing out her cherries equally.

8. Repeat 7, but with different numbers of cherries.

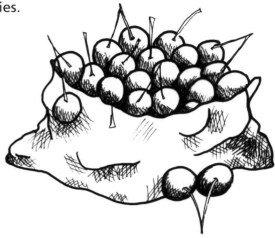

Acting out

Acting out problems is a fun way of thinking about the skills needed to solve them. It helps the children think about the information that they are being given and how to use it to work through the problem. Give groups of children a short problem, some time to work out their scene and any necessary equipment, e.g. paper, pens, coins, books, Unifix cubes, plasticine – anything which will help them. Then ask them to mime their problem, using any pictures and props that they want to use. The rest of the class need to work out what the scene is all about and what the problem and its solution are.

This activity is an effective one to do with all age ranges. Below are some ideas that can be adapted to suit your particular class simply by altering the numbers.

Examples

1. Sam, Adam, Jenny, Peter and Jane are having a picnic. Peter has brought 20 biscuits to share equally with them all.
   How many will they each have?

The group needs to have five children in it. Preparation by the children beforehand could involve using paper to cut 20 circles with biscuit or 'B' written on each to represent the biscuits. They could begin their mime by sitting down and pretending to eat. The child who is playing Peter could share out the circles among the others. Then each child could stand up in turn and show how many biscuits they have.
The children will probably come up with some great ideas of their own.

2. Andrew, Fatima, Tomas and Steph have been given 26 sweets. Andrew shares them out equally.
   How many will be left over?

3. Eric ran 4km; Catherine ran twice as far.
   How far did Catherine run?

4. Mr Smith has grown six tomato plants. On each plant there are six tomatoes. *How many tomatoes has he grown altogether?*

5. My mum shared £6.40 equally between my brother, two sisters and me. *How much were we each given?*

6. Tammy and her friends went to the shop and bought a loaf of bread for 60p and some milk for 45p. They gave the shopkeeper a £5 note. *How much change did they receive?*

7. At my friend's house, there are two adults, three children and four puppies. *How many legs are there?*

8. My dad drove us all to the seaside. It took 2 hours 15 minutes. We left at 9am. *At what time did we arrive?*

Making up

Asking the children to make up a variety of problems from numbers or facts is a helpful way of encouraging them to think about relevant information, which operations to use and how to solve two-step problems. It enables them to put problems into a context that is meaningful to them and therefore easier for them to understand. When using this type of activity, it is essential to discuss with the children as a class the work they have done, asking such things as how they thought the problem could be solved, whether there was any redundant information and how many steps they thought were required to achieve an answer.

During a plenary on another topic, make the exercise relevant to the objectives of the lesson.

For example, if the objective for the lesson was to 'write a subtraction statement corresponding to a given addition statement', the plenary may involve writing up the numbers 20, 14, 34 and asking the children to make up some addition and subtraction problems using them – including one of the numbers as the answer:

Examples
There are 20 girls in our class and 14 boys. *How many are there in the class altogether?*

There are 34 children in our class but 14 are away. *How many are present?*

My friend baked 34 cakes; she burnt 20. *How many were not burnt?*

Esther had 14 posters of her favourite band; Ian had 20 of his. *How many did they have between them?*

In this case it is important to make reference to the inversion aspect from the objective during discussion of the problem work.

Write these numbers on the board: 12, 4, 6, 1

Give the children a few minutes to think of a problem involving those numbers.

They could work in pairs or small groups, or if you prefer individually. Pairs or small groups will give support to any who are not so confident, especially if doing this kind of activity for the first time. Discuss the problems with the class. Encourage the use of a variety of operations, e.g. group 1 make up a problem involving addition, group 2 subtraction, group 3 a mixture of multiplication and subtraction, group 4 a mixture of division and addition. This could be carried out according to ability.

Possible problems

Arsenal played Manchester Utd. on Saturday and won 12 goals to 6. They played Sunderland on Sunday and lost 1 goal to 4.
How many goals did Arsenal score altogether?

Mr Spago baked a pizza and cut it into 12 pieces. He gave four pieces to his family, six to his neighbours and ate one himself.
How many pieces of pizza were left?

Sally had four boxes of eggs. Each box contained six eggs. She used 12 eggs to make breakfast for her Scout group and dropped one.
How many did she have left?

Paul had 12 sweets; he put them into four piles, ate one from each pile and was then given six more to add to each pile.
How many were in each pile?

Other examples

1. **How many …?**   **54 cakes**   **63 biscuits**

   We baked 54 cakes and 63 biscuits for the school fair.
   How many things did we bake altogether?

   The baker sold 17 loaves of bread, four doughnuts, 54 cakes and 63 biscuits this morning in his shop.
   How many more biscuits than cakes did he sell?

2. **32**   **8**   **divide**

   I had 32 stickers. I divided them equally among eight children.
   How many did they each have?

   At the barbecue my friend cooked 32 sausages. There were enough for eight sausages each.
   How many people were at the barbecue?

3.   **£3   £2.50   £6.95   58p**

My mum collected money for a charity. At one house someone gave her £3, at another £2.50, at the third £6.95 and at the last 58p.
How much did she collect altogether?

Sarah went to the market. She bought some flowers costing £3, a pack of batteries costing £2.50 and a shirt costing £6.95. She had 58p left.
How much money did she start off with?

4.   **3 hours 20 minutes $^3/_4$ hour**

My family and I went to visit some friends at the seaside. We set off at 9am. It took us 3 hours and 20 minutes to get there. We were $^3/_4$ of an hour late.
At what time did our friends expect us to arrive?

Peter started his homework at 4:30. It took him 3 hours and 20 minutes to finish it. He had a break of $^3/_4$ of an hour at 5:30. When he had finished he had his supper.
At what time did he have his supper?

5.   **15   24   8   9**

Possible problems:
We went to the zoo and saw 15 monkeys, 24 penguins, eight giraffes and nine camels.
How many animals did we see altogether?

We went to the circus and saw 15 horses, 24 clowns, eight acrobats and nine trapeze artists.
How many more clowns were there than acrobats?

6.   **75cms   1.15m**

Katie was growing a sunflower. When she first measured it, it was 75cms tall.
Next time she measured it, it was I.15m taller.
How tall was it?

I made a really long worm out of plasticine. It was 75cms long. I then stretched it until it measured 1.15m.
How much longer had I made my worm?

Playing games

Here are three simple games that you may find useful to have up your sleeve for the occasional plenary session. They can be adapted to use for any topic.

The Grid Game or Bingo

The idea of this game is for the children to fill in their own grids (of any size) with numbers or shapes or whatever is relevant to the lesson. You then call out types of numbers or properties of shapes. If they have any that are applicable to what you have said, they cross it out. The winner is the first player to cross out all their numbers, as in the following example.

~~18~~	~~28~~	12
32	24	16
9	27	3

Children fill their grid with numbers multiples of 3 and 4. Call out times table questions: 6 x 3, 7 x 4 etc. If the children have the answer on their grid they cross it out.

Other ideas could be:
a) Numbers from 10 to 100: ask vocabulary-based statements – multiples of 10, 5 and 2, even numbers and odd numbers.
b) Any three-digit numbers: they cross out any number they have written that has the digit that you call out in the position you call it, i.e. if they have written 256 and you say 5 in the tens or 50, they cross that out.
c) Any 2-D shapes (drawn): make statements to do with their properties, e.g. cross out all the shapes that are quadrilaterals, any that have three corners, any that have at least one right angle.

Ladders and Snakes or In the Bin

This game can also fit in with virtually any topic you might be studying. You will need a selection of around 20 cards with suitable numbers on, such as:

Odd numbers from 1 to 100: write these numbers on the cards. Pick the cards randomly, and as each one is drawn, call it out; the children need to write it in a rectangle of the ladder. The aim is to fill up the ladder with numbers ordered from lowest at the bottom to highest at the top. Any that won't fit go into the snake. For example:

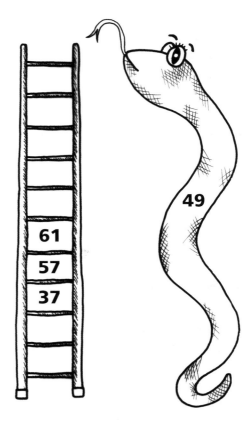

> **Odd numbers from 1 to 100:**
>
> **57 picked, put on 4th section.**
>
> **61 and 37 picked, put on ladder.**
>
> **49 picked, no room, goes in snake**

You can use photocopiable sheet 11 for this activity.

Play your cards right

Great fun! This game follows similar rules to the television game show. It allows for much questioning and it is important to do plenty of this to make the most of the game.
You will need to make about 20 cards with numbers on to do with a particular topic, e.g. multiples of 5. The children need to predict whether the next card will be higher or lower than the preceding number. They need to predict five in a row correctly. The class could play as a whole group, however it can be more exciting if you divide them into two teams.

Photocopiable Sheet 11
Ladders and snakes

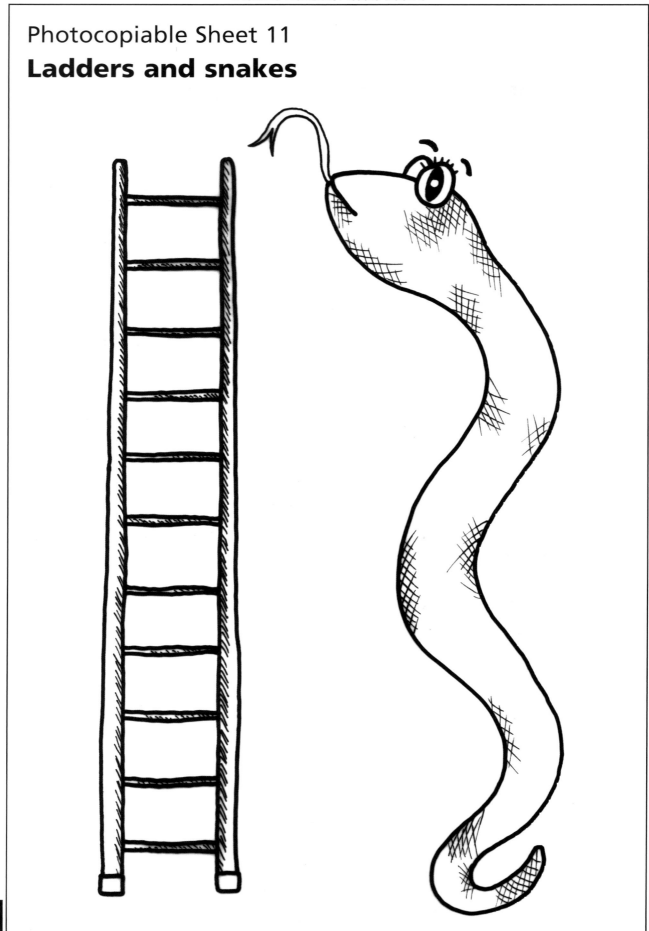

© The Questions Publishing Company Ltd

Chapter 5
Other ideas for an effective plenary

Analysing the lesson

Ask the children how they found the lesson. Was it easy or difficult? What was the most enjoyable part? Which was their favourite 'bit'?. Focus on one of these aspects during one plenary and another, another time.

1. Record their comments on the 'easy' parts as if brainstorming:

Year 4 example

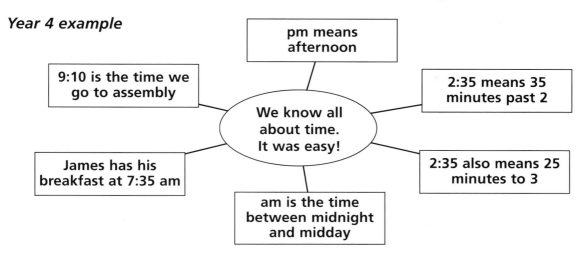

2. Have a vote to find out which was the most enjoyable part of the lesson and why. Use that information to build a bar graph with the class.

Year 3 example
Story problems involving money

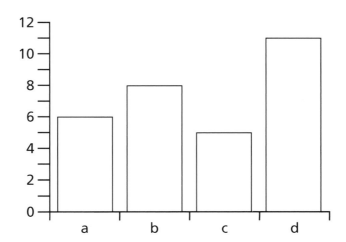

Children's comments:
a   "I enjoyed answering the problems." So did five others.
b   "I enjoyed looking for the relevant information." So did seven others.
c   "I enjoyed making up my own problems." So did four others.
d   "I enjoyed working with my partner." So did ten others.

Invite some children to come to the board to construct the bar graph and add the labels.

3. Make a display of one of the children's favourite parts of the lesson. This can be used later as a prompt when the subject next comes up.

Year 4 example
Shape and space problems
Make some statements on card or paper and invite a few children to match them with appropriate pictures.

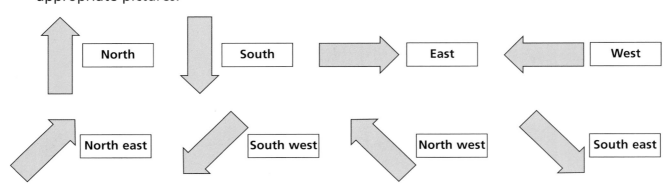

4. Discuss the most difficult part of the lesson, find out what made it so and where the children have a particular problem. This is not the occasion to try to sort out any problems as it may well take more time than is available, but make a note so that you can work on them again the following day or whenever is most appropriate. Make a poster to show who has a difficulty and with what. Only do this if there is a large group of children with the same feeling and follow that up with another poster when they have succeeded.

Year 3 example

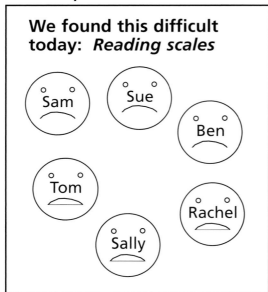

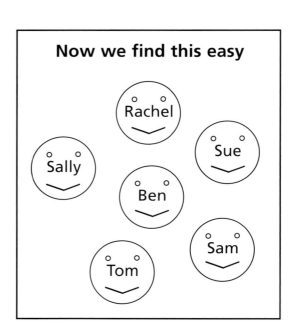

Identifying misconceptions

The above ideas help to identify any misconceptions that have occurred. If these are minor ones that can easily be sorted out, deal with them during the plenary. If they are more complicated, make a note of them and deal with them next time you meet for maths. However, if you notice during individual, paired or group work that there is a problem or misconception most of the class are having, or common errors are being made, stop the lesson and go straight into a 'plenary' for the rest of the session in order to sort it out.

Making general rules

Children should be helped to generalise a rule from examples generated by different groups.

Examples
1. You can add consecutive numbers by doubling one and adding or taking away one.
2. To multiplying by 20, multiply by 10 and then double.
3. All four-sided shapes are called quadrilaterals.
4. Multiplying any numbers together can be done in any order.
5. An even number is always the sum of two odd numbers.
6. You can often solve calculations in division by using multiplication.

Reflection

You can use this to draw together what has been learned, reflect on what was important in the lesson, summarise key facts, ideas and vocabulary and what needs to be remembered. This needs to be discussion based. There should be lots of interaction with the children, asking them appropriate questions, listening to them talking about their work and discussing what they think is the important aspect to remember. Summarising key facts, ideas and objectives is an important part of this type of plenary, as is the reviewing of the vocabulary that the children should have learnt.

Drawing it together

This needs to be a discussion-based session. Once again, there should be lots of interaction with the children, asking appropriate questions and listening to them talking about their work. At the end of a unit it is important to draw together what has been learnt over the series of lessons by summarising key facts, ideas and objectives.

Consolidating and developing

During the plenary session, recap what has been learnt briefly and then develop the work a stage further, for example:
1. After a Year 3 lesson ordering numbers up to 1000 using cards, review and then move on to plotting them on a blank number line.
2. Following a very practical Year 4 lesson on measuring liquids in calibrated containers, begin rounding to the nearest 100 ml.

Celebrate success in the children's work

Discuss with the children whether they think they have been successful during their group or whole-class work in achieving the objective of the lesson. Ask for comments as to why they think they have succeeded and ask them to give an example of the work they have completed. Then try one of the following:

1. Invite other children to say something positive to the child, pair or group about their particular success.
2. Give the child/pair/group a clap.
3. Have a success poster or sheet on the wall and write that success and the children's names beside it, e.g.

> ## This week we are learning to identify right angles in shapes.
>
> Ali, Ben, Susie and Jo know squares and rectangles have four right angles.
>
> Katie now knows that a regular pentagon has no right angles.

Add to this over the week and continue with it next time the topic is revisited, so that every child will see their name on the chart over a period of time. Add any small success: this is particularly important for those children who lack confidence.

4. Award points or merits for success, possibly displaying them on a poster, e.g.

5. At the end of a topic, if the children have worked well and achieved success, have a celebration 'party', playing lots of maths games and having a drink and biscuit. Create a special plenary by inviting other children or the head of the school along to share these successes with them.

Number cards A

0	1	2	3
4	5	6	7
8	9	10	11
12	13	14	15
16	17	18	19
20	21	22	23

Number cards B

24	**25**	**26**	**27**
28	**29**	**30**	**31**
32	**33**	**34**	**35**
36	**37**	**38**	**39**
40	**41**	**42**	**43**
44	**45**		

Days of the week

Monday

Tuesday

Wednesday

Thursday

Friday

Saturday

Sunday

Months of the year

January	**February**
March	**April**
May	**June**
July	**August**
September	**October**
November	**December**